Ancient Peoples and Places

CHINA

General Editor

DR GLYN DANIEL

Ancient Peoples and Places

CHINA

BEFORE THE HAN DYNASTY

William Watson

77 PHOTOGRAPHS
65 LINE DRAWINGS
AND 3 MAPS

FREDERICK A. PRAEGER
New York

THIS IS VOLUME TWENTY-THREE IN THE SERIES

Ancient Peoples and Places

GENERAL EDITOR: DR GLYN DANIEL

BOOKS THAT MATTER *Published in the United States of America in 1961 by Frederick A. Praeger, Inc. Publisher, 64 University Place New York 3, N.Y. All rights reserved Library of Congress Catalog Card Number: 61-14105 © William Watson 1961 Printed in Great Britain*

CONTENTS

ILLUSTRATIONS

7

9

Introduction

U NLIKE SOME NATIONS described in the books of the present series, the Chinese people is not difficult to define historically. It has occupied the valley of the Yellow river from time immemorial. Even the Palaeolithic race, whose bones have been found there, shares some physical peculiarities with the present inhabitants. While the archaeologist may point out culture-traits which connect with other regions, he discovers no evidence of tribal movements from without of a size and coherence likely to determine thenceforth the racial and cultural constitution of the land. The manner and the time of the colonisation of the great Central Plain of north China, sup-posing such a thing were ever a definable historical event, is beyond knowledge and conjecture alike.

Within the larger sphere of eastern Asia the Chinese people as we know it today is better defined by language and culture than in anthropological terms. In general a distinction of the physical type may be observed north and south of the Yangtze river, a boundary which corresponded in early times to a cul-tural division between the relatively advanced civilisation of the Central Plain and the more primitive south. The popula-tion north of this line, black-haired and brown-eyed, is com-paratively taller and much of it has the Mongol characteristics of yellow skin, slanting eyes and prominent cheek-bones. But other individuals are lighter of skin, with rounder eyes and flatter cheek-bones. In the south the average height is less, the skin is browner and the Mongol characteristics are rarer.

We may assume that the periodic infiltration of tribes from the north into the settled region of the river valley, a constant theme in the early histories which caused anxiety to Chinese rulers for thousands of years, had begun long before these barbarians appeared as a threat to the Shang state in the second half of the second millennium B.C. The result of this contact is reflected in physical traits in some groups of the north Chinese population which relate them to the Turkish, Tibetan and Tungusic races. In the south anthropologists speak of a similar admixture of elements belonging characteristically to the peoples of south-east Asia. In both areas it is assumed that these extraneous racial elements fused with an autochthonous Chinese stock, though the definition of a pure Chinese strain seems to elude anthropologists, and, fortunately for the theme of this book, has no bearing on cultural history. The distinctions noticeable today are no greater than those existing in any great race of multiple origins, and similarities preponderate over local differences. It is clear, however, that the expansion of the Chinese southwards in the past (culturally the process may be observed from Neolithic times) displaced as well as absorbed peoples of somewhat different ethnic character. The Miao and Lolo of south-west China surviving at the present day as 'national minorities' are unsinicised remainders of a population which once covered the whole of the southern region. History records that peoples allied to these, no longer distinguishable from the Chinese population, once occupied territory farther east than their present home.

Neolithic and Bronze Age civilisation first arose in China in the region extending westwards from the coast approximately between the 35th and 40th parallels of latitude, comprising the lower and middle course of the Yellow river as far as its abrupt northward turn on the boundary of Shensi province, thence extending westwards along the Wei river valley into the river basins of central Kansu. To the north and south this zone is well defined. The alluvial plain of Hopei is bounded by quasi-steppe land on the north, while the northern tracts of Shansi, Shensi and Kansu pass into desert. Kansu is mountain-locked to west and south, and the succession of east–

west mountain ranges (Pei Ling Shan, Ch'in Ling Shan, Huai Ling Shan) continuing eastwards through Shensi and Honan marks the southern limit of this primary cultural area. In the south-east, where the mountain line ceases, the land is drained into the river Huai, and here the low-lying tracts around the lower Yangtze, rich in lakes and marsh, are easily accessible from the Central Plain.

The region we have defined coincides approximately with the distribution of the loess, a fine, compact and permeable soil, fertile and easily worked, which is believed to have been carried by wind from hither Asia during the Pleistocene period as a concomitant of the climatic changes which produced the glaciations of the Ice Age. In Kansu it lies in great depth, often exceeding 200 feet, and in places is eroded into fantastic narrow ravines. The regime of erosion and the sudden heavy rains which cause it, cease as we pass eastwards through Shensi pro-vince, and from the junctions of the Wei with the Yellow river begins the Central Plain proper. Here the loess has been redeposited by soil-sated rivers which ever tend to raise their beds above the level of the plain and spread their fertilising floods. This is the region where uncontrollable flooding has caused periodic disasters throughout Chinese history—and where the greater possibilities of irrigation have helped the farmer with the problem of watering the porous loess. On the loess territory of both kinds flourished the Neolithic cultures of north China, though we shall note differences between the remains found in the area of primary loess and in the Central Plain. The natural route of expansion lay in the south-east towards the mouth of the Yangtze.

The western edge of the Central Plain follows the line of the T'ai Hang range, which descends from the far north and divides off the high parallel valleys which constitute the province of Shansi. The same grassed and well-watered ter-rain continues westwards into Shensi. To judge from the occurrence of sites, this upland area was less frequented by the Neolithic farmers; although no less suitable for millet and bar'ley, it was more favourable than the plain for grazing horses. It was the home of the Chou people, the ultimate conquerors of the Shang.

South of the Shensi plateau the line of the Ch'in Ling Shan beyond the Wei river begins the succession of high mountain chains which bar the way to the mountain'locked, flatter area of Szechwan, whose rivers drain into the Yangtze. The Neo'lithic culture of Szechwan connects with a tradition extending along the Yangtze valley, and borders with the Neolithic tradition of the Central Plain only at its extension into Anhui province and the Huai river basin. To the west rise the all but impenetrable mountains of Yunnan and Sikang which separate China from Burma and the Tibetan plateau.

The south and south'east of China beyond the Yangtze is a region of frequent low hills, still better wooded than the north, and in early times probably covered with dense forest inimical to agriculture and long resistant to the penetration of cultural influences from the north. Civilisation spread slowly there from the middle of the first millennium B.C. Only in the last century B.C. were Chinese armies moving freely on the southern seaboard.

The purpose of this book is to give a brief account of the material culture of ancient China as revealed by archaeological study. It is well to recognise at the start that the familiar suc'cession of Stone, Bronze and Iron Ages and their subdivisions are less clearly definable in China than in Europe, where this system of archaeological classification was evolved. We shall often have occasion to point this contrast with the West. If Neolithic culture is defined as a farming economy practised exclusively with stone tools, then we may say that large tracts of China remained in a Neolithic Age long after the discovery of bronze and even survived for some time after iron had become the normal material for tools in the most advanced parts of the country. What is more mysterious in the light of the early economic history of the West, iron itself was slow to replace bronze in the manufacture of weapons. Bronze-casting first appears in a form which would correspond in the West to a relatively advanced stage of the technique, having many points comparable to the 'Late Bronze Age' of Europe; and iron was cast some centuries before it was forged, thus confounding our Western preconception of the natural development of this technique. The period here designated the Later Bronze Age comprises also a stage equivalent to the Early Iron Age of Europe.

Western archaeologists were surprised to learn of these departures from the cultural sequence established by long study in the West. They were sometimes inclined to account for it by supposing that China had been subjected to the same kind of acculturation from without that so often determined the course of events in Central and Northern Europe. Here in-fluences spreading ultimately from the higher civilisations of the Near East and the Mediterranean, at particular times and by determinable routes, created fairly well defined and intelli-gible cultural successions. The development of culture in China did not depend on such parcels of external influence. To Chinese archaeologists it appears unnecessary to stress the evidence against diffusionist views which brought civilisation to China from Egypt, Mesopotamia or the Caucasus.

We should also note at the outset that a description of early China that is confined to information which the archaeologist can provide, and disregards the literary tradition, necessarily forgoes much that the latter can contribute to cultural history. For example, we get a jejune picture of the lives of the Neo-lithic and Bronze Age farmers unless we take into account peasants' songs which were anthologised in literary and

usually moralised dress in the Shih Ching, the 'Book of Odes'.
This work reached its present form between the ninth and
fifth centuries B.C. The material is basically traditional and
must in part reflect customs descending from a much earlier
period, some possibly from Neolithic times. The harvest and
mating customs and village festivals which it celebrates conjure
up pictures of colourful life in well-organised rural communities.
But the archaeologist and historian is naturally shy of drawing
on facts recorded at so comparatively late a time, to illustrate the
background of cultures which his excavated evidence places in
a much earlier period. But in the interest of strict history there is
a compensating advantage. If the archaeologist is silent before
the theory that the spiral patterns on certain Neolithic pottery
represent the movements of a fertility dance, he can on the other
hand point out that archaeological research lends no support
to the tradition of a highly civilised Hsia dynasty which begins
the dynastic succession of traditional history. He can question,
for example, the statement sometimes made that the Chou
dynasts by their conquest of Central China in the eleventh
century B.C. were responsible for introducing the use of the
plough, or the practice of burying the great under high mounds,
or, on more general grounds, that the peoples of the Chou confederacy were mere barbarians before their conquest of the
Shang brought them into contact with a higher civilisation.

The mention of the Hsia dynasty, the very existence of which
some modern Chinese historians have questioned, introduces
us to an aspect of Chinese historical writing which is at once
the delight and the despair of any who attempt to reconstruct
the beginnings of Chinese civilisation. In the last few centuries
of the Chou period and under the earlier Han dynasty, i.e.
from the fifth to the first centuries B.C., Chinese historians were
dominated by a view of the past consecrated in the philosophy
of Confucius and his followers. From the beginning, it was
held, all China had been ruled by emperors. The list is headed

by a group of rulers of impossible longevity, credited with the heroic feats of culture-heroes, and rationalised in a spirit which seems drily mundane in comparison with Western mytho-logies. Persons of myth are turned into Emperors and ministers engaged in practical administration. Thereafter follow the 'Three Dynasties' of Chinese historians, the houses of Hsia, Shang and Chou. The exact dates attributed to all the emperors were not questioned before the second century B.C., when the historian Ssü-ma Ch'ien recorded that his sources did not vouch for their accuracy before a date corresponding to 841 B.C., which remains the earliest year of the exact chronology.

The political theory of Confucian historians required that China should have at all times been subject to a single ruler. It is possible that the Hsia dynasty, to which so much doubt attaches, was contemporary with that of Shang rather than its predecessor, though the excavated inscriptions by which the historicity of the Shang state was fully corroborated, give no hint of Hsia. The differing accounts of the legendary period reflect theories current in the last few centuries B.C. The ortho-dox list names nine pre-Hsia rulers, beginning with T'ai Hao, said to have occupied the throne from 2852 B.C. They are made to correspond in various ways with a group of Three Sovereigns and a group of Five Rulers, the names of these differing from the dynastic ones, and regarded as personal appellations. The Three Sovereigns were mostly identified as Fu Hsi, inventor of writing and cooking and patron of hunt-ing; Shen Nung, the farmer-god; Sui Jen, inventor of fire. Huang Ti, the Yellow Emperor, may figure among them. All or some of these, and other legendary personages, are found variously combined in different texts.

One may surmise that tribes inhabiting different parts of the country contributed the stories of their ancestral gods and animistic lore to the general stock of Chinese legend, although small traces remain of local connexions. Huang Ti and Yen Ti (the latter identified with the farmer-god Shen Nung) are connected in legend with rivers in the western province of Shensi, where they are said to have spent their youth. Huang Ti had a fight with a 'rebel' Ch'ih Yu in the neighbouring province of Shansi. Slight hints are traced of connexions of others of the legendary rulers with east China, the lower basin of the Yellow river and the Huai river valley. These local allegiances correspond approximately to the two cultural traditions found in north China in the Neolithic period.

Indications of geography preserved in Chinese flood legends not unnaturally point to the region around the mouth of the Yellow river. The emperor Yü, regarded as founder of the Hsia dynasty, is credited with mastering a flood which threatened the whole country with destruction and with the invention of systems of river control. The same feat is credited to the founder of the following dynasty of Shang. Scattered references to another flood-hero called Kung Kung are confused, leaving us uncertain whether he started the flood, stopped it or unintentionally aggravated it. Kung Kung is remembered best for his fight with Chuan Hsiu for control of the empire. In the struggle he ran his head against Fu Chou, the mountain which in Chinese myth corresponds to the heaven-supporting central pillar of the Shamanistic cosmologies of east and south-east Asia. This pillar was bent, and consequently the heavens were tilted lower in the north-west, causing the stars to move from east to north-west and the rivers to flow in the opposite direction.

The conventional history generally takes no account of creation myths, but part of one such myth was adopted and assigned a place at the beginning of the story. This tells of the emperor Kao Hsin who accepted the services of P'an Ku, described as a 'dog of five colours', in overcoming the bar-barians of the south. P'an Ku was rewarded with the gift of Kao Hsin's wife, and their descendants peopled the southern region. The accounts of P'an Ku vary like all the other stories. He is also said to have emerged from chaos and in dying to have given birth to the universe. Part of his history is localised in Hunan, once the home of the non-Chinese Miao tribes who eventually were displaced farther to the south-west. The admission of this alien myth into the Chinese pseudo-history was probably a counterpart to the expansion of Chinese power and civilisation at a relatively late date into the 'unopened' region south of the Yangtze river.

In the pseudo-historical schemes the legendary rulers might be assigned a remote place in space as well as time, being described as celestial emperors controlling the four quarters of heaven. They were sometimes paired with four spirits who appear in Han art symbolised by the White Tiger of the west, the Green Dragon of the east, the Red Bird of the south and the Dark Warrior of the north, this last being oddly repre- sented as a serpent in copulation with a tortoise. When the Five Rulers are associated with the Five Elements of earth, fire, water, wood and metal they appear annexed to a natural philosophy which marks the beginning of Chinese science.

The bureaucratic character with which official historians were at pains to endow legendary figures is in keeping with the attitude to the past taught by Confucius. After his death in 479 B.C. his followers continued to interpret selected passages of myth in the interest of their own moral and political teach- ing. Confucius himself had taken the early dynasts of the house of Chou as his exemplars, and from the earlier legendary emperors chose Yao and Shun (two of the Five Rulers) for special praise. Shun's simple peasant virtue had caused him to be adopted by Yao as his successor and he thus fitly symbolised the promotion by merit in the public service which Confucius so ardently advocated. It is characteristic of Chinese myth- making that Yao was regarded among other things as the ancestor of potters, and Shun of foresters.

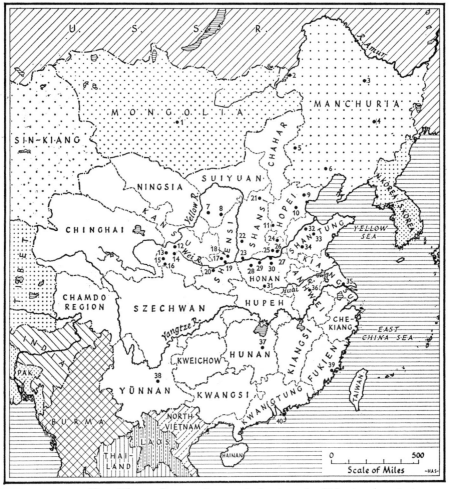

Fig. 1 The modern provinces and location of chief sites named in text

MONGOLIA

I SHARABAKH-USU

MANCHURIA (NORTH-EAST
CHINA, PROVINCES OF HEILUNG-
CHIANG, KIRIN, LIAONING, JEHOL)

2 DJALAI NOR

3 ANG ANG HSI

4 KU HSIANG TS'UN

5 LIN HSI

6 HSING LUNG HSIEN

SUIYUAN

7 SHUI T'UNG KOU

8 SJARA OSSO GOL

Soon an interest in material relics of the great days of Chou arose, and set the pattern for the antiquarianism which has persisted in China to the present time. This interest attached almost exclusively to the bronzes and jades associated with the official ritual which Confucianists advocated as a guarantee of political stability. The volume of Chinese antiquarian writing on such objects, and usages connected with them, exceeds anything of the kind in other literatures. Yet it seems that nothing approaching a historical classification of antiquities was attempted before the twelfth century. The methods of archaeological research developed in Europe in the nineteenth century reached China as part of the intellectual revolution which overthrew the old order in China only half a century ago.

HOPEI
9 T'ANG SHAN (CHIA KO CHUANG)
10 CHOU K'OU TIEN
11 HAN TAN (CHAO WANG CH'ENG)

KANSU
12 PAI TAO KOU P'ING
13 MA CHIA YAO
14 HSIN TIEN
15 PAN SHAN
16 MA CH'ANG

SHENSI
17 PAN P'O TS'UN
18 P'U TU TS'UN
19 CH'ANG AN
20 TOU CHI T'AI

SHANSI
21 LI YÜ
22 TING TS'UN
23 SHANG TS'UN LING

HONAN
24 ANYANG (HSIAO T'UN, HSI PEI KANG, WU KUAN TS'UN, TA SSŬ K'UNG)

25 HSIN TS'UN
26 HUI HSIEN
27 CHENG CHOU
28 SHENG CH'IH HSIEN
29 LOYANG
30 HSIN CHENG
31 HSIN YANG

SHANTUNG
32 CH'ENG TZŬ YAI
33 LIN TZŬ
34 CH'Ü FU

KIANGSU
35 YEN TUN SHAN

ANHWEI
36 SHOU HSEIN

HUNAN
37 CH'ANG SHA

YÜNNAN
38 SHIH CHAI SHAN

FUKIEN
39 T'AN SHIH SHAN
40 HONG KONG

Chapter I

The Palaeolithic and Neolithic Periods

CHOU K'OU TIEN

THE CHINESE ARCHAEOLOGICAL SITE best known to the western world is Chou K'ou Tien, where the first skull of *Pithecanthropus pekinensis*, Peking Man, was found in 1929.[1] It is situated 26 miles south-west of Peking, where the easternmost extension of the Western Hills sinks into the Hopei plain. Immediately west of the village rises a hill, about 60 metres high, much of which has now been destroyed by quarrying. In the earlier Pleistocene period the general level of the plain was some 60–70 metres above the modern surface, and the Chou K'ou Tien hill is the remains of one of the pockets of limestone which were scattered over it. Large fissures in the rock were gradually filled with stony rubble and red clay. It was excavation in these deposits that brought to light animal and human bones, together with the signs of human habitation—roughly fashioned stone tools, burnt bones and the ashes of hearths. The connexion of the human fossils with the products of man immediately gave the site a unique interest, for previously the finds of human bones of comparable age (for example, the Swanscombe skull from the middle gravels of the Thames estuary) had not been so directly related to artifacts and other evidence of human activity. It is now generally agreed that the Chou K'ou Tien deposits from which the human bones were recovered are not of lower Pleistocene date, as was once believed, but of the middle Pleistocene, and therefore of approximately the same age—estimated at about half a million years—as the earliest human bones and artifacts discovered in England, Europe and Africa.

Pithecanthropus pekinensis, or *Sinanthropus,* had much the same primitive physiognomy as his near-contemporaries in Europe and Africa. His head differed from a modern skull by its low forehead and small capacity, which was about two-thirds of the average size of the modern brain-box. His jaw was prominent but his chin fleeting. A heavy eyebrow ridge depressed the upper edge of the eye sockets into an irregular line. He stood upright, with a stature of about 1·56 metres, little different from the average of the modern population of the same region. Some of his minor physical characteristics have persisted in the same region through a period of time equal to an appreciable fraction of the whole duration of the human race. He shares his broad nose, high cheek-bones and a shovel-shaped depression on the inner face of his incisors with the modern population of Mongolia and northern China. In the Chou K'ou Tien remains no variation of the physical type is noticeable throughout the 50-metres depth of deposits known as Locality 1, which are thought to represent a period of some hundreds of thousands of years. From the conformation of the skull it has been surmised that *Sinanthropus* was capable of articulate speech. He evidently enjoyed corporate life. In the total of forty-five individuals represented by the bones found thus far at the site both males and females are present. Fifteen of them were children.

The materials which *Sinanthropus* used for making his tools were chiefly a hard green sandstone, limestone, quartz and quartzite, all less suited to shaping by percussion than flint and chert, of which only small quantities were present in the deposits. The forms of the flint and chert tools are, however, close enough to those made from the less tractable stones to show that the differences between them and the Palaeolithic tools of Europe and Africa do not arise merely from the greater difficulty of working a less suitable material, but spring from a different cultural tradition. Tools were found in Localities 13, 1 and 15, of which the first is the oldest and the last the latest, both corresponding to the middle Pleistocene. Locality 13, which seems not to have been regularly occupied, produced a single piece, a small chopping‑tool made from a pebble, which is the earliest sign of man unearthed so far in China. The animal fossils which accompanied it indicate that Locality 13 was inhabited at a time following the establishment of the modern river system in the Yellow river basin. Near the tool lay some broken stones foreign to the deposits filling the rock fissures, and a few burnt bones.

Fig. 2a

The bulk of the stone tools found at Chou K'ou Tien came from Locality 1, where they lay near the human bones. Many of them are so roughly shaped that only the foreignness of their material and the frequency of their characteristic shapes demon‑strate that they are not natural products. The commonest form is a heavy, flattish stone, up to six or seven inches in length, more or less round or oval, on which a crude cutting edge has been contrived by striking off irregular stumpy flakes. One side is generally left smooth—it is often the pebble sur‑face—to give a good grip for the hand. The flaking may extend to as much as two thirds of the perimeter of the tool, and flakes may have been struck from both sides of the edge, though this last is rare. An occasional specimen is more carefully shaped by the removal of regularly spaced, smaller (but still deep‑biting) flakes from both sides of the working edge, which consequently has a zigzag line.

Fig 2b

In addition to these 'core‑tools' Locality 1 produced num‑erous smaller pieces, scrapers and points measuring an inch or two in length, in which the tool is formed from a flake struck from a larger lump of stone. Such 'flake‑tools' have generally received further trimming at the edge, which is thereby strengthened, the fracture‑surface of the original flake being left smooth. Some of these more refined implements show signs of use.

The climatic environment in which Peking man lived may be judged from the kinds of animal bones found lying close to the human relics in Locality 1. They included those of the sabre-toothed tiger, water-loving species such as an otter and a water-buffalo, grazing animals such as buffalo, deer and sheep; and wild pig and rhinoceros which could only be at home in thick vegetation, though the species of camel suggests that more arid terrain was not far distant. It seems that a north temperate climate prevailed, with fairly long winters. It is probable that Peking man lived at the time of one of the interglacials of the Pleistocene period, possibly the earliest or Günz-Mindel interglacial, which corresponds in Europe to the early phase of the Acheulian culture of skilfully fashioned flint 'hand-axes'.

But the Acheulian tradition of stone-working, which is found as far eastwards as southern India, is distinct from the tradition represented at Chou K'ou Tien. The latter is more closely related to a stone industry found in north-western India, in which a 'chopper-tool' of less regular design takes the place of the hand-axe. This broad division of techniques may reflect a racial division of ancient humanity inhabiting opposite ends of Asia. As far as the level of intelligence im-plied by the two techniques is concerned there is no reason to set one above the other, particularly if we compare the Chou K'ou Tien tools with the early Acheulian (Abbevillian) of France, and make allowance for the difference of materials used.

Locality 15 is a fissure about 70 metres from Locality 1. Its filling of earth and rock debris contained traces of ash, many animal bones and a number of tools of a new kind. The tools are made of a smooth-textured flint, 'sinian chert', of which only some rare pieces occurred at Locality 1. Both the forms of the tools and the species of animals represented by the bones suggest that Locality 15 is the later site, though it is still dated geologically to the middle Pleistocene.

Many tools made from small flakes were recovered at Locality 15. Their skilful retouching and more purposeful shapes are a sure sign of technical progress. Roughly sym-metrical points are trimmed at the edge by minute deep-biting

Fig. 2c

flakes ('step-flaking'), or by narrow and shallow flakes resembling the 'pressure-flaking' first practised in Europe in the
more evolved stage of the Acheulian culture. Sometimes the
trimming is carried over both sides of the point. A few triangular flakes have been struck from cores of flint on which
the back of the piece destined to be struck off received some
preliminary shaping—there is no sign of this degree of fore-
thought among the tools of Locality 1. No human bones were
found, but since the stone technique appears to be a further
development of the technique practised at Locality 1, their
makers may have belonged to the same race. The site was
inhabited by men at a time when the temperate climate indicated by the fossils from Locality 1 had given way to cooler,
semi-arid conditions with desert still close.

Throughout his long occupation of the natural caves at
Chou K'ou Tien *Sinanthropus* was a hunter and ate mainly
venison. The great number of split bones he left in his midden
show his liking for marrow and some split human limb bones
and skulls treated in the same way suggest that he was not
averse from cannibalism. He was capable of killing the swift
gazelle and wild horse, a hunt which presupposes a capacity
for group organisation. His social life was of a brutish kind.
He has left no relics which hint that he practised any art or
magic, or even show that he buried his dead.

The signs of technical advance perceptible in the stone tools
from Locality 15 are repeated at a site in Shansi province, near

Fig. 2d

Ting Ts'un. The geological stratum from which chert tools
and three human teeth were recovered is a gravel bed belonging
to a series widely distributed in northern China. It lies below
the red and yellow soils of the loess, of which the great central
plain of China is composed, and is held to be equivalent to the
period in which the filling of the Chou K'ou Tien fissures was
accumulated. The species of animal bones found in the gravel
suggest a time rather later than the occupation of Locality 1

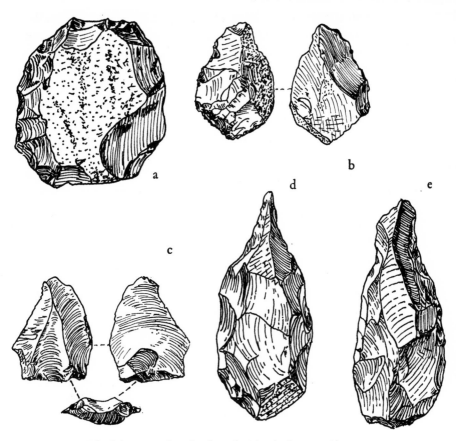

Fig. 2 *Palaeolithic stone tools: a, b, Chou K'ou Tien, locality 1; c, Chou K'ou Tien, locality 15; d, e, Ting Ts'un. Scale 1:3*

at Chou K'ou Tien and closer to the date of Locality 15, and the forms of the stone tools point in the same direction. The human teeth from Ting Ts'un (one incisor and two molars) are intermediate between those of *Sinanthropus* and modern man. The incisor has the shovel-shaped depression on its inner face. The most fully formed stone tools are some thick points of triangular section and about 6 inches long. They have a superficial resemblance to the hand-axes of the West, but the working of the stone is less well controlled than in the best Acheulian specimens. The remaining tools are smaller, neatly struck flakes with one trimmed edge. In some cases there is a suggestion, as at Locality 15, of preliminary work executed on the core before the flake was struck off.

The chance which has preserved for us at Chou K'ou Tien a stratified deposit of animal fossils, human bones and artifacts accumulated over long periods in the life of a distinct community is not encountered again in the archaeological record before the Neolithic period. Between the latest relics of *Sinanthropus* at Chou K'ou Tien and the earliest trace of food producers along the course of the Yellow river some hundreds of thousands of years must have passed. In contrast to the corresponding period in Europe, which is the age of Mousterian man and the famous cave-artists of the Upper Palaeolithic, in China the later Palaeolithic cultures are little known. Here the latest division of the Pleistocene period, equivalent to the great series of Würm glaciations elsewhere, is marked by the deposition of the loess over the northern half of the country. One can imagine nothing more discouraging for human life than the regime of powerful dry and cold winds which geologists believe to have carried the blanket of loess from periglacial regions lying far to the north-west. Vegetation and animal life must have all but vanished for long ages, and with them the little groups of men.

OTHER PALAEO/LITHIC SITES   This severe climate had its milder intervals however, and some human handiwork attributable to this period shows that the vital technique of stone working was taking the same general trend in eastern Asia as is to be observed in the West. At Shui Tung Kou in the Ordos, the tract of desert lying within the great northward loop of the upper Yellow River, flint implements were excavated together with animal bones and the charcoal of camp-fires from a point 12 metres below the surface and near to the base of the loessic soil. The tools are made of simply chipped pebbles, or, more rarely, of long flakes, a little more refined than the handiwork of *Sinanthropus*. These are the relics of hunters of small game, notably wild ass, antelope and ostrich. At Sjara Osso Gol on the southern bor- *Fig. 3a* der of the Ordos region, signs of habitation were discovered some 50 metres below the present grassland, in a geological environment which points to a terrain of small lakes and sand dunes. Here the yield of animal bones was specially rich. Species of ostrich, elephant, rhinoceros, deer, horse and goat all witness to a relatively damp climate and to well-forested land as well as prairie. The majority of the stone tools, flake points and scrapers trimmed on a single face, are smaller than those found at Shui Tung Kou and are more skilfully made. Among them were found small, roughly conical cores of chert from which narrow parallel-sided blades about an inch long had been skilfully struck in succession. No examples of the small blades themselves were found, but they are sufficiently attested by the parent cores. They are similar to the tiny tools—microliths—first manufactured in Europe in the Magdalenian culture of the late Upper Palaeolithic period and thereafter in the Mesolithic cultures which preceded the rise of the Neolithic. In the West these blades were mounted in rows in handles of bone and wood, and we may suppose that the same idea was followed in China.

A stone industry comparable to that of Sjara Osso Gol, though without the microliths, was practised by the inhabitants of a cave situated near the summit of the hill of Chou K'ou Tien. 'Upper Cave Man' is represented by the skeletons of ten individuals all of the modern type, *Homo sapiens*. Bone and horn implements accompanied the flints, and some ground and drilled stone beads painted red with haematite, bone pendants, perforated and polished shell ornaments show an advance of sensibility over his *Sinanthropus* predecessors. The scattering of haematite around one of the skeletons indicates a deliberate burial, indeed is the earliest instance of a funeral rite which was to persist in China through the Neolithic period and into the Bronze Age. There is proof too of trade over considerable distances. The haematite must have come from Lung Kuan, beyond the mountains a hundred miles to the north. The marine shells must have travelled at least 120 miles, from the nearest part of the coast, and one large fresh-water species is thought to have been brought from beyond the Yellow river, over 200 miles away. The skulls have mixed features, some Mongoloid and others declared to be akin to modern Esquimaux and Melanesians.

This latest material recovered at Chou K'ou Tien is taken to mark the end of the Palaeolithic period. Its date can only be roughly estimated, lying perhaps between 30,000 and 20,000 years B.C. Thereafter, and before the rise of the bronze-using civilisation of central China in the second millennium B.C., human activity is recorded in finds of stone tools and potsherds at small surface sites scattered through the vast region of desert and grassland of Mongolia, Manchuria and the Ordos. The archaeologist's great problem is to determine whether such traces of habitation in this northern region are all contemporary with the Neolithic cultures of China—the relics of hunting tribes who copied the pottery of their farming neighbours—or in part are older than any of the farming communities. It is tempting, perhaps rational, to assume that these surface finds are the traces of long-enduring hunting communities who were ultimately affected by the farmers of the Yellow river, possibly some of them themselves providing the farming population. So far however archaeologists have found no predecessors for the farmers of the Yellow river valley, no sites on the Central Plain to bridge the gap between Upper Cave Man and the Neolithic villages. We cannot even affirm that the sites on the

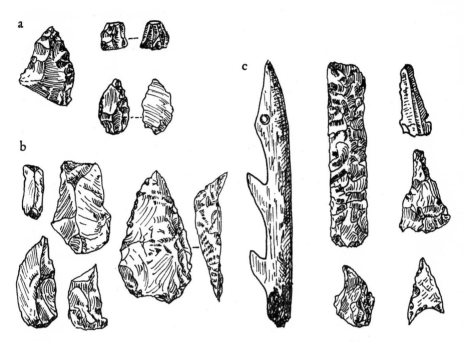

Fig. 3 Mesolithic tools: a, stone flakes and core, Sjara Osso Gol; b, stone flakes, Ta Li Sha Yuan Region, Ordos; c, bone harpoon, stone knife, gravers and arrowhead, Ang Ang Hsi. Scale 1:2

Gobi desert precede the Neolithic villages in time, and that there is not a similar gap all over Mongolia and Manchuria.

The Gobi desert which now stretches across the southern half of Mongolia is for the most part an uninhabitable region of shifting sand. But numerous depressions on its surface are surrounded by ancient consolidated dunes which show that many more lakes existed there formerly than survive at the present time. Rain was more abundant and the desiccation which has now driven out plants and animals had not reached so far. The stone implements of prehistoric man are generally found on or near the ancient dunes, marking habitation or

MICROLITHIC CULTURES IN THE GOBI DESERT, MONGOLIA AND MANCHURIA camping places once located near water. The Sino-Swedish expedition of 1927–35 discovered 327 sites between Manchuria and Sinkiang. Even allowing for the long period of time which the sites may cover, the density of population which they reflect was considerable by the standards of primitive hunting peoples. On many of the sites flint microlithic tools were found mixed with polished or partly polished stone tools and often fragments of pottery, which all the world over are the hallmarks of Neolithic culture, or at least denote close contact with farming communities. But the apparent contemporaneity of Mesolithic and Neolithic techniques may in some instances be illusory. The erosion by wind of the sandy terrain probably tended to gather the material in pockets on the surface—this phenomenon has been noted elsewhere—and mixed together relics of different ages which in other geological circumstances would have been preserved stratified at different levels. Only at Shabarakh Usu, one of the 180 sites discovered by the American Central Asiatic Expedition of 1922–30, could it be affirmed that Neolithic remains were at a higher level than the Mesolithic.

The most characteristic of the Gobi stone tools are the microliths made from small flakes struck serially from the core. Besides flint and chert they were made of jasper and other coloured fine-grained stone. The flakes were neatly trimmed to make points and blades of irregular shapes. They are a little finer than the microliths of much earlier date found at Sjara Osso Gol and like them were probably intended to be set in rows to edge cutting tools or to barb spears. The cores remaining from the flaking of the tiny blades were mostly cylindrical or conical, the cylindrical ones spread throughout the region and the conical predominating in east Mongolia and Manchuria. Such cores are characteristic of the Mesolithic cultures of Europe and North Africa, but whereas in the West the flakes obtained from them were often trimmed into neat geometrical

Fig. 3b

shapes—crescents, triangles and trapezes—those of eastern Asia have no such regular outlines.

The southern limit of the distribution of the microlithic sites appears to lie along the Nan Shan, Alashan and Yin Shan mountains, which separate the Gobi desert from the drainage basin of the Yellow river and its tributaries. The sites are found, however, beyond the mountains and the river in the Ordos region and eastwards in Manchuria beyond the considerable barrier presented by the northsouth range of the Hsing An mountains. More than geographical obstacles must have checked their spread to the south. If the barrier was 'human rather than natural', as Chêng Tek'un suggests, we must suppose that it was raised by the farming communities of the Yellow river valley, and that the Mesolithic hunters of the Gobi were their contemporaries. Once settled farming was established in the Central Plain cultural separation of peoples north and south of the mountain line is understandable. The cultural boundary which emerges in history as the conflict of the Bronze Age states of northern China with the turbulent nomadic tribesmen of the Mongolian grasslands was already drawn in Neolithic times.

The material of Neolithic type found together with the flaked implements and microliths in Mongolia and Manchuria consists of polished or partly polished stone axes and pottery. The polished axes are chiefly of the rounded type which finds parallels in Siberia to the north and northwest, though some pieces resembling the axes of northern China with squared crosssection have also been collected. Apart from rare perforated stones which some interpret rather dubiously as weights for digging sticks, there is no evidence for tillage. The polished rectangular or crescentic stone knives which accompany neolithic remains everywhere in northern and central China are unknown beyond the northern margin of the Yellow river basin. This fact alone suggests that settled farming was

Fig. 4

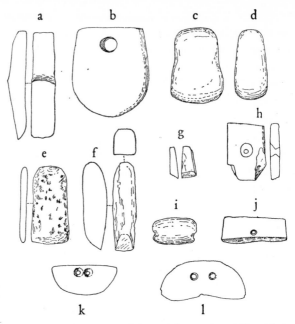

Fig. 4 Stone axes and knives of the Neolithic period: a, Ch'ing Chiang, Kiangsi; b, Lien Kang, Kiangsu; c, d, Pan P'o Ts'un Shensi; e, f, g, Jih Chao, Shantung; h, Ch'eng Tzŭ Yai, Shantung; i, Yang Shao, Honan; j, Shang Lu Ts'un, Honan; k, Lu Shun Yang T'ou Wa, Liaoning; l, Ch'ih Feng Hung Shan, Jehol. Scale 1:6

never practised in the northern region, and tends to disprove the theory that the nomadic stock-raising found there in his, torical times descends from a full farming economy which degenerated into nomadism as the grasslands became desert.

The pottery found on the Mongolian sites is all hand-made and differs somewhat in the northern and southern zones. In Outer Mongolia is found a reddish or grey ware, plain for the most part but sometimes bearing incised or stamped geometric designs. Southwards in Inner Mongolia similar rough sherds appear along with others of more refined make, which add

burnishing, red pigment and applied bands of pie-crust ornament to the methods of decoration. A few specimens of the
legs of tripod bowls have been collected. This superior pottery
and particularly the tripods, which parallel the ubiquitous *ting*
of the Neolithic of northern China, undoubtedly reflect the
influence of the farming culture of the Yellow river valley.
The rougher ware is generically similar to pottery found in
Siberia.

At the eastern end of the northern region the few sites so far
investigated reveal a similar mixture of mesolithic and neolithic elements. At Djalainor, close to the Hsing An range on
its Manchurian side, were found flint and quartzite tools of the
Gobi type and a single squared piece of polished stone, but
polished axes were absent. Two pieces of deer antler, one with
an annular groove and another bored with two holes at right
angles have been tentatively regarded as hafting attachments
for stone axes in the manner practised in the West in the Swiss
lake villages. The remains of some interwoven willow sticks
have been thought to be a fish trap, and indication of a lake-side
fishing village. At Ku Hsiang T'un on the Manchurian side of
the mountain there were further signs of lake-side habitation in
the geological strata. At Ang Ang Hsi in Heilungchiang,   *Fig. 3c*
northern Manchuria, some barbed harpoon-heads were excavated, quite similar to those used in the latest Palaeolithic
and the Mesolithic of western Europe. They furnish even better
evidence for the importance of fishing. Here a small polished
axe resembles those made in the West for hafting by means of a
socket of deer antler. No specimen of such a socket was recovered but the existence of other handles of bone makes it
likely that such a device was in use.

In some other fundamental respects the material from Manchuria and eastern Mongolia differs from the characteristic
equipment of the Gobi sites, and points to a connexion with
the north-east. At Ang Ang Hsi triangular and leaf-shaped

arrowheads were found in quantity, some with hafting tangs, and all trimmed by neat pressure flaking of a kind not encountered farther west in Mongolia. There was an abundance of coarse grey and reddish pottery, among it some intact vessels. The villagers buried their dead under heaps of earth near their settlement, including in the graves pottery vessels, bone and stone tools and in one instance a dog. Both the cultural remains and the geological strata which contained them point to a later date than that at Djalainor, and suggest that the Ang Ang Hsi settlement belongs to the Neolithic period. Farther south, at Lin Hsi in Jehol province a similar though more advanced pottery was found, some of it wheel-turned, and here cropping is attested by spatulate stone hoes and part of a stone reaping knife.

Over this whole area where microliths are found there is no sign of settled agricultural life. In the Yellow river valley there is no trace of a population slowly evolving an agricultural economy, for between 'Upper Cave Man' and the farming villages of the full Neolithic the archaeological record is blank. The germ of the Neolithic revolution, the knowledge of cropping and cattle-raising may, indeed must, have come through the northern region from some other part of Asia. It is asking too much of coincidence to assume that such a fundamental revolution as had already occurred in the Fertile Crescent of the Near East should have happened independently a second time in China. The passage of ideas, whether the form of a tool or the method of making it, or knowledge of the advantages of food production need not leave cultural remains on its path. There can be no question of the migration into China of large numbers of farming tribes bringing with them a complete cultural complex. Had this happened it would be difficult to explain how the Neolithic culture of the Yellow River valley and the Central Plain came to be divided into distinct traditions, one reaching to the north-west and the other to the north-east. This regional difference corresponds in a general way with the division we have noted between the Gobi and Man/churia, which may mean that its roots go back beyond the Neolithic period altogether. The two neolithic traditions over/lap in central China, and the north/eastern is there demon/strably later. But they both are possessed of a fully developed agricultural economy. Neither yields to the other in the excel/lence of pottery, the large size of villages or skill in polishing stone tools. Nor does either appear to be the parent of the other.[2]

The Neolithic culture of central and north/western China is named Yang Shao, after a village in Sheng Ch'ih Hsien, Honan province, where Andersson first identified it in 1922. Its remains are characterised by grey and reddish pottery; a finer pottery with painted decoration; thick polished stone axes which are generally oblong with a rectangular or rounded/rectangular section; oblong reaping knives made of thin plaques of stone polished and pierced for hafting; stone and clay spindle whorls; and tanged arrowheads of polished stone. The distribution of the sites is confined to the loess area and follows in the main a broad east–west line along the middle course of the Yellow river in Honan and southern Shansi, and the valley of the Wei river leading across the middle of Shensi into the upper basin of the Yellow river and its tri/butaries in Kansu. From central Honan, where the sites are most frequent, the Yang Shao area extends south into the Honan plain towards the upper waters of the river Huai, and northwards sites occur in the flat and well/watered tract lying either side of the boundary between the provinces of Hopei and Shansi. In choosing places for settlement the Yang Shao farmers avoided mountainous and even upland territory, keeping to the well/drained and rich agricultural soil of the plain near rivers.

In Shensi and Kansu the erosion of the thick loess deposit has formed at intervals deep, mazy ravines with vertical walls

THE YANG SHAO NEO/LITHIC CULTURE

rising sometimes to heights of hundreds of feet. Here sites have been found on terraces well above the flood plain of the streams. It is impossible to be certain that the apparent eleva᷍tion above the valley bottom was as great in ancient times as it is today, though it is probable that the peculiarity of loess erosion was much the same then as it is at the present time. Both the primary and the redeposited loess are equally fertile, but the difficulty of watering fields in the ravined region of the primary loess must have been a serious handicap to the agriculturalist, and the dissected terrain an obstacle to com᷍munication. We shall note divergencies in the neolithic material from the two areas which reflect this difference of environment and suggest that the western branch of the Yang Shao culture was comparatively isolated and conservative—a distinction which to some implies a cultural division within a broader tradition.

The picture of neolithic life which emerges from the study of the remains is one familiar to archaeologists. Groups of farmers lived in settled communities in undefended or lightly defended villages near rivers, sometimes choosing slightly rising ground— in the plain this could only mean a few feet above the general level—to escape the seasonal flooding. Their chief grain was millet (*Setaria italica* (*L*) *Beauv*), traces of which have been recovered at Wang Yung Ching Ts'un in Shansi and Pan P'o Ts'un in Shensi. How far rice cultivation entered into the Yang Shao economy we cannot say at present, but some rice᷍grain impressions on a potsherd unearthed by Andersson at Yang Shao Ts'un prove that it was not unknown. We must suppose the Yang Shao villagers capable of the careful organisation which the planting and irrigation of rice fields calls for.

These villages differed from comparable ones in the late Neo᷍lithic period of southern Russia or even those of the Late Bronze and Iron Ages of southern England chiefly by their greater size: the populousness of the Yellow river valley must have equalled that of ancient Egypt and Mesopotamia. In some cases the neolithic village seems to have been even greater in extent than the modern villages standing near their sites. The remains found at Hua Yin Hsi Kuan P'u in Shensi were spread over an area of more than 900,000 square metres, representing presumably an agglomeration of villages. The neolithic strata at some sites reaches a depth of 5 metres. But only one village site, at Pan P'o Ts'un near Si⁄an in Shensi province, has been excavated so far with the thoroughness which affords a toler⁄ably complete picture of the village scene.

At Pan P'o Ts'un round and oblong hut foundations were uncovered, set close together and lying a few feet below the ancient land surface. Some of the foundations overlapped, at one place five floors superimposed one over the other were evidence of long occupation, new buildings having been erected over the ruins of the earlier. The timbers of the huts had naturally all perished, but traces of the post holes preserved in the soil told something of their structure. The round huts measured about 5 metres in diameter; one still retained around the edge of the sunken floor a wall about a foot high made of clay mixed with grass, and the floor had been sealed with a coat of limy earth. Outside the wall a circle of post holes indicated supports for the eaves of the roof. Posts had stood inside the house in rows of three on either side of a central clay⁄built stove. These provided the main support for the roof, which is thought to have been planked with wood on the underside, and together with the circle of slenderer posts set around the wall suggest an over⁄all conical shape, the steeply sloping sides reaching almost to the ground at the eaves. Two rows of slender posts at the entrance showed how this shape required the door to be set some distance inside the perimeter of the house. The clay debris which strewed the floors of most of the huts seems to have been the outer covering of the roof. Storage

Plate 1

Plate 2

Plate 4

Fig. 5

spaces and ovens were formed inside the houses by excavating in the soil and lining the recess with fine clay. They can be seen against both walls of the larger rectangular building shown on Plate 4. Near the houses were found a number of storage pits, some rounded at the bottom and with narrow mouths, others, which appear to belong to the later period of the site, were some 6 metres deep and lined with a layer of burnt clay. The pits were filled with grey habitation earth in which were mixed fragments of pottery, stone tools, ashes and animals' bones. In one part of the village were found the remains of six clay-built kilns, five of them consisting of cylindrical chambers about a yard wide and three yards long, provided with flues to conduct the flame from the fire in the forward end of the kiln to the firing chamber at the back. In one of the kilns stood several unfired coarse pots.

The pottery found at Pan P'o Ts'un is characteristic of the wares of the centre of the Yang Shao area. The principal shapes are deep jars with slightly everted rim, bowls with flat or rounded bottoms, tripod bowls (*ting*) and amphorae with

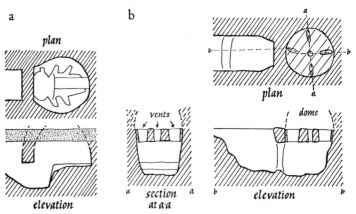

Fig. 5 *Pottery kilns at Cheng Chou: a, Yang Shao culture at Lien Shan Pi; b, Late Shang period, at Pi Sha King. Diameters of pottery kilns approx. 1 m.*

narrow neck and pointed base. The finest ware is red, well levigated, of a hardness which must have required a firing temperature of 1000 degrees centigrade or more—a heat easily attainable in the kilns described. The light-grey pottery is almost equally fine in texture, though softer. In the coarser reddish and grey potteries the clay is mixed with coarse sand. The hard red pottery is often burnished and painted with geo-metric patterns in black resembling those found farther east, though the schematic designs of a fish and a human face found at Pan Po Ts'un are exceptional. Elsewhere only a timid bird's head is occasionally introduced. The rougher pots are plain or incised with simple geometric pattern, or impressed by cords or matting.

Plate 5

The analysis of local divergencies in Yang Shao pottery has not yet been taken very far, but since the variation of pottery shapes and ornament may indicate where the culture is to be looked for in its earliest form and in which directions it spread, it is important to note what local differences are already appar-ent. It is clear that judged by its pottery the Yang Shao culture does not present the same unified character as is found in some of the migrating cultures which spread through the forest zone of Europe at the beginning of the Neolithic period. The local variation in the pottery suggests that the Yang Shao culture developed in northern China and argues against any pro-found influence from outside.

Fig. 6

The most distinct branch is that of the western extremity of the area, where sites are distinguished as belonging to a 'Kansu Yang-shao' culture, or the Pan Shan culture. It is best known from the painted funerary urns from four ancient cemeteries on hills—the Pan Shan—in the Ning Ting district of Kansu. They were first collected by Andersson in 1923. After his discovery, the sites were exploited by the local inhabitants and yielded the splendid funerary urns which began to reach Western museums a generation ago. The large urns are nearly

THE KANSU
NEOLITHIC
CULTURE

Fig. 7

Plate 6

globular in shape, on a flat base, with an out-turned low lip or a short tubular neck, and generally furnished with lug handles at the neck or on the sides. Their red fabric is similar to the finest described from Pan Po Ts'un; but their decoration, like their shapes, is quite distinct. On them iron and manganese pigment is used to produce black, red and brown in combina-tion, applied on the burnished surface in a rich variety of spiral, wave-shaped, rhomboid and many other geometric pat-terns of great beauty. The ornament is set in zones and panels, the lighter colour often outlined by a darker line with dog-tooth serrations on the inner side—the 'death pattern', as Andersson named it in recognition of the funerary character of the vessels. The urns, like all the Yang Shao ware, are hand made, though trued at the mouth on some turning device simpler than a fast-revolving potter's wheel. The excellence of the pottery and the splendour of the decoration makes these urns the most attractive product of the Chinese Neolithic.

Andersson's researches established a chronological series of painted pottery cultures in Kansu. After the Pan Shan group he places another termed Ma Ch'ang, from a site in the T'ao river valley, which seems to derive from it, its pot shapes and painted patterns marking a degeneration of the tradition which produced the great funerary urns. The Ma Ch'ang vessels were also made for burial, but at Ma Chia Yao, a short distance away, a habitation site was discovered. A few potsherds of the Ma Ch'ang type were unearthed here, showing that the two sites were roughly contemporary. The great bulk of the pottery, however, was different and its shapes and decoration are much closer to the painted Yang Shao ware of the Central Plain, though they do not reproduce it exactly. The latest stage is that of the Hsin Tien graves, whose painted pottery shows a further decline. A few bronze ornaments from these graves prove that the painted pottery tradition survived at least into the beginning of the Bronze Age.

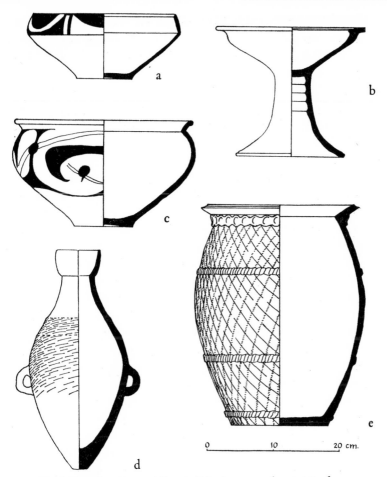

Fig. 6 Yang Shao Pottery. The painted bowls a, c are characteristic of the Central Plain. The amphora d is found mainly in Shansi. Scale approx. 1:6

A problem which still awaits satisfactory solution is the relationship of the Kansu painted ware to that of the Central Plain. The contrast between the two regions goes further than the pottery. The Kansu tombs contained small chisels of jade

43

and cylindrical marble beads which are not found elsewhere, though the jade rings and crescentic pendants can be paralleled by stone and clay versions of neolithic date in central China. These objects are in fact an intimate link with the culture of the Central Plain, for they survive there into the Bronze Age and are then made of jade: they are the *pi*ring and *huang*crescent, ritual forms which are later interpreted as cosmic symbols, and which were made and buried with the dead down to Han times.

Plate 3
There is also a difference in the burial rite. In Kansu the body was laid on the right side with the legs bent, and facing a row of pots in which meat and grain were placed; or the body was laid prone, or the bones were gathered after the body had decayed, and reburied. The burial customs of the eastern Yang Shao province are known best from Pan P'o Ts'un. Here the adults were buried lying extended on the back in rectangular pits which were sometimes lined with wooden planks, and children were buried in large clay urns. This difference in the funeral rite was to survive into the Bronze Age.

Yang Shao sites of the eastern type extend westwards along the valley of the Wei river, and on the upper reaches of the river in Kansu they are situated only about two score miles east from the site of Ma Chia Yao. Between the two areas— that of Ma Chia Yao which links with the Pan Shan-Ma Ch'ang complex, and the sites of Li Hsien and Tien Shui Hsien marking the penetration of the eastern tradition into Kansu—passes the watershed dividing the T'ao river from the upper waters of the Wei.

Although thirty years have passed since Andersson made his survey, still not enough is known of the exact chronology and distribution of the two variants of Yang Shao culture to assess the importance of this boundary. Apart from the unique funeral urns of Pan Shan and Ma Ch'ang the domestic potteries, for all their broad similarity, reveal tantalising differences

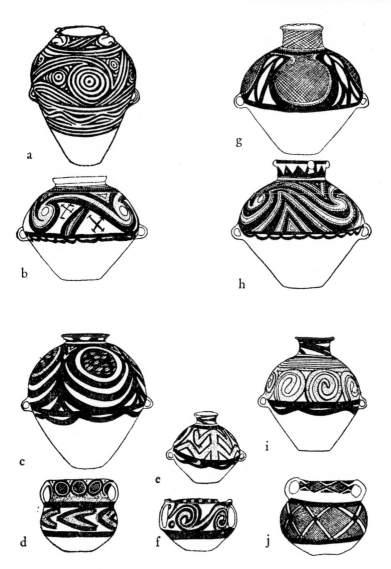

Fig. 7 Painted pottery of the Kansu Yang Shao culture: a–d, Pan Shan type; e–j, Ma Ch'ang type. Scale approx. 1:16

45

Fig. 6a, c

Fig. 7f

when they are compared closely. The ware of the eastern Yang Shao is red while that of Ma Chia Yao is buff. The former combines black and red paint in the ornament, and the latter uses them apart. Only the eastern pottery makes use of a white slip. The Ma Chia Yao bowls are painted inside and on the outer lip, and those of the east only on the outer sides. The geo-metric motifs of the decoration, mainly lines and concave-sided triangles in both areas, are distinct in style. The running spirals and summary birds and animals of the Kansu ware are not known in the Central Plain, nor the tall urns with narrow mouth which were found at Ma Chia Yao.

The similarity of some of the decoration of the Chinese painted ware to that of some Far Western potteries is equally puzzling. For example, burial urns of the southern Russian Tripolye culture with their ornament of elaborate black spirals, urns with black and red spirals excavated at the Bronze Age site of Trialeti in the Caucasus, and similar pots from the Bronze Age city of Anau in Turkestan, all are surprisingly like the Pan Shan and Ma Ch'ang urns. But the theory of a great migration which introduced these urns and with them Neolithic culture into China from the Far West has been very sceptically received, not least by Andersson himself.

Andersson points out that such parallels of decorative motifs between the Chinese and the Western pottery are closest in the Ma Ch'ang stage and not in the Pan Shan stage, although it is the earlier: 'In the Ma Ch'ang time, when the decorative style was already in decline, there developed strong parallels on the one hand to Anau, and on the other to Tripolye. With our present limited knowledge it is premature to discuss where these cultural impulses first arose and how they migrated across Central Asia.' We are left to conclude that the small beginnings of the painted pottery tradition of China may have been in-spired from the West, but its flourishing period, that of Ma Ch'ang and the Yang Shao sites of the Central Plain, was an

Fig. 8 Painted pottery head. Kansu Yang Shao culture. Ht. 6½ ins. Scale 1:3

independent growth, the work of Chinese and not of immi‑ grants from the West.

The dates estimated by Andersson for the painted potteries remain uncontested, and are not likely to be made more precise until much more has been excavated and perhaps the techni‑ que of Carbon 14 measurement can be applied. He placed the Pan Shan stage between 2200 and 1700 B.C., and the Ma Ch'ang stage from 1700 to 1300 B.C. The Yang Shao of the Central Plain, since it overlaps in time with Ma Ch'ang, would occupy the first half of the second millennium B.C.; but it must have ended by about 1500 B.C. Then it was supplanted by the culture of the Shang Bronze Age, when painted pottery was abandoned.[3]

The earliest date of the eastern painted pottery is still un‑ known. If the Pan Shan stage preceded it, as Andersson is inclined to think, we must assume that Neolithic culture arose earlier in the river valleys of Kansu than in the Central Plain. This is intrinsically improbable. The Pan Shan urns may be a local and isolated development, not much earlier than the Ma Ch'ang stage and no more than contemporary with the beginning of the Yang Shao culture on the middle course of the Yellow river.

From Honan to the east and north-east stretches the domain of a different Neolithic tradition, the Lung Shan culture. In Honan at least it can be shown to be later than that of Yang Shao, for at a number of sites in this densely inhabited part of the Central Plain Lung Shan pottery has been found strati-fied above Yang Shao remains and below the Bronze Age level. The Yang Shao and the Lung Shan cultures and a more primitive tradition in south-east China comprise the main divisions of Neolithic China. These are based primarily on differences in the potteries found on their sites. If stone tools, methods of burial or types of habitation are taken as criteria, the cultural map is considerably changed. The distribution of variants of these features does not coincide with the geographical limits of the most characteristic potteries. Before we proceed with the description of Neolithic culture lying outside the Yang Shao sphere we may glance at the geographical distribution of one important implement which disregards pottery frontiers: stone reaping-knives. These might be regarded as the type fossil of the Chinese Neolithic.

Fig. 9

In the only considerable study of this kind which has been undertaken An Chih-min distinguishes three types of such knives: all of which are about 6 inches long and 2 or 3 inches wide.[4] The roughest kind, approximately oblong, has generally a notch for hafting at each narrow end. Its distribution follows the line of the painted pottery sites from Kansu, along the Wei river valley and the middle course of the Yellow river as far as Honan. A thinner, better polished knife of crescentic shape, pierced with a hafting hole or two holes set close together in the middle and generally nearer to one edge, covers the north-east, from southern Manchuria, through Hopei and Shantung and Honan as far as the upper waters of the Huai river in the southern part of this province. A few have been found in

Fig. 4

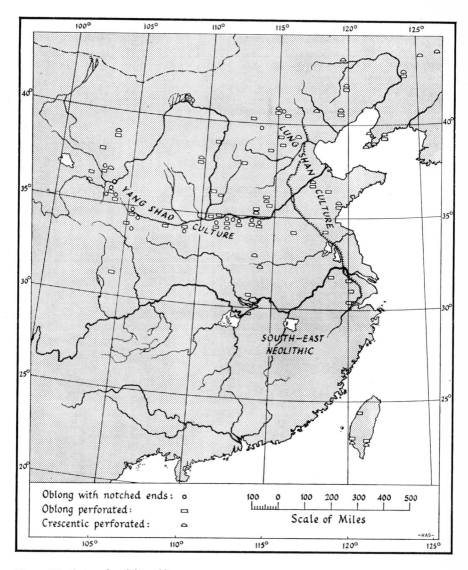

Fig. 9 Distribution of neolithic sickles

Shansi and northern Kansu, but it is only in Honan that the area of the second type coincides with that of the first. The third type of reaping/knife is oblong, but thinner, more regular and better ground than the first and it is pierced with one or two holes. This type occurs over an area which embraces the whole distribution of the other two with the exception of Shantung and the extreme north/west.

While the crescentic knife is characteristic of the Lung Shan culture of the north/east and the finer oblong type of the Yang Shao culture, their geographical distribution takes them well beyond the areas in which the most characteristic potteries of these cultures are found. The crescentic knife occurs with pot/tery of the south/east Neolithic in Kiangsu province and the oblong type spread as far south as the Yangtze. The pierced oblong knife survived into the Bronze Age in the hands of farmers following their unaltered neolithic way of life, and was eventually copied in iron.

The distribution of sites attributed to the Lung Shan culture lies through the coastal region from Hopei to Chekiang and extends inland into Honan. Some of the villages were of sizes comparable to those of the Yang Shao communities, but generally they seem to have been smaller, ranging from a few hundred to a hundred thousand square metres, and occupying low knolls or river terraces. Their houses were little different from those we have described from Pan P'o Ts'un, sunk in the earth, the floors often coated with lime, and both round and rectangular in plan. They buried their dead in earth pits, ex/tended supine or prone and accompanied by pots, axes and arrows. Their animals were the pig, cow and goat. The abundance of stone reaping/knives found on the sites is evi/dence for their agriculture, but the species of grain which they cultivated is not known. Their stone axes are generally of oblong shape, thinner and broader than those of Yang Shao and are often pierced near the centre of the upper half. Much

Fig. 4

use was made of shell for knives and scrapers. At many sites, particularly in the southern area of the Lung Shan region, mounds of shells of fresh-water molluscs show that this source of food was of greater importance here than it was to the Neo-lithic communities farther inland.

The most distinctive of the Lung Shan potteries is a ware *Fig. 10* of black fabric with a well smoothed, often lustrous surface obtained by burnishing. For fineness and finish it compares well with the black Athenian pottery of the fifth to fourth centuries B.C. If any external dressing was used to produce the gloss, it is not detectable after firing. The vessels are wheel-turned and sometimes reduced to a thickness of less than an eighth of an inch. The handled cups, bowls and deep goblets generally have straight sides, sloping or vertical, giving an angular outline unusual in pottery which is not deliberately copying metal vessels. No metal has ever been found, however, associated with Lung Shan remains. The surface of this fine ware is left undecorated, but the grey ware and the coarse sandy pottery which makes up the bulk of the fragments at Lung Shan sites often bears incised and stamped ornament of a simple geometric kind. The regional variation of the pottery types is greater than in the Yang Shao culture of central China and demonstrates even more convincingly the difficulty of finding simple typological definitions for two neolithic tradi-tions.

To the south, sites classed as Lung Shan contain an in-creasing quantity of the rough brown ware characteristic of the south-east Neolithic, just as the increasing number of shell mounds show that the population relied increasingly on food gathering, and less on corn and cattle. Inland from Shantung towards Honan there is found a greater proportion of grey pottery indistinguishable from the coarse ware of the Yang Shao sites; the fine black pottery becomes rarer. Grey and brown pottery decorated all over with impressions of twisted cords, which is less prominent in Shantung and Hopei, is here the commonest ware. When a site contains only this rough pottery, it may be uncertain whether it should be classified as Yang Shao, Lung Shan, or even whether it belongs to the earlier Bronze Age, for the grey pottery tradition survives in central China into the Shang period.

Deposits of the Lung Shan culture have been found at Anyang, the site of the future Bronze Age capital, stratified above the Yang Shao level and below the Bronze Age level; and Lung Shan pottery has been found beneath the earliest Bronze Age remains in central Honan at the Bronze Age city of Cheng Chou. The connexion between the Bronze Age culture of the Shang kings and the Lung Shan Neolithic *Fig. 10a, f* is evidently very close. It is borne out by the similarity of some of the earliest bronze vessels—notably the three-lobed *li* tripod and the tripod *chia* goblet to the Lung Shan pottery types, and by the flat stone axes of the Lung Shan kind which continued in use in Shang times. Moreover, oracle-taking by cracking bone with heat, which was crucial in Shang religion, was practised in a cruder fashion at the Lung Shan type site of Ch'eng Tzŭ Yai in Shantung.

The distribution of the most individual traits of the Lung Shan culture show that important influences bearing on the Bronze Age civilisation of the central provinces originated in the north-east, in the area comprising the provinces of Shantung and Hopei. The fine black pottery, which is the most striking technical achievement of the Lung Shang Neolithic, is commonest in Hopei and western Shantung, and by comparison very rare in Honan. The strange vessel called *k'uei*, a *Fig. 10e* tall jug with the lower part expanded into three large legs like goat's dugs, has a similar distribution. Conversely the *li* is much commoner in Honan. There is no suggestion in this of the total replacement of one social group by another in the Central Plain, or of the violent interruption of cultural

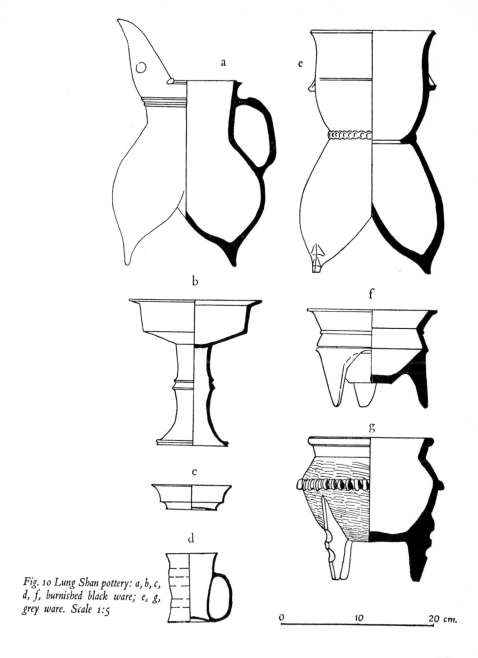

Fig. 10 Lung Shan pottery: a, b, c, d, f, burnished black ware; e, g, grey ware. Scale 1:5

0   10   20 cm.

traditions established when the Yang Shao farmers formed their first settlements.

As we pursue the Lung Shan sites southwards from Shan-tung through Anhui province and the coastal provinces of Kiangsu and Chekiang, the same attenuation of the most characteristic Lung Shan features occurs. Coarse corded pottery predominates. Along the valley of the Yangtze, from Szechwan to the sea, it is associated with sites established on eminences near to rivers and lakes. Although much neolithic material has been collected from this region, where the pre-sence of the *li* and the stone reaping-knife connect the origin of agricultural life with the Neolithic cultures of the Central Plain, little can yet be said of the stages of cultural development in this area and in the vast hilly region of southern China. The thick forest which must have covered the south in pre-historic times would be a serious obstacle to the spread of farming. Isolated groups of agriculturalists, themselves still much depending on the hunt, must have been scattered among tribes of hunters whose methods had advanced little beyond that of their palaeolithic forebears. It must suffice here to note that the neolithic communities of southern China were heirs to traditions of stone-craft quite distinct from those of the north. Just as stone industries of mesolithic type practised in Kuangsi province are related to the Hoabinhian culture of Indochina, owing nothing to the northern microlithic tradi-tion, so the quest for parallels to some of the polished stone tools of neolithic type—notably a tanged or double-shouldered axe—leads south-westwards into Burma and the Malay peninsula.

The dating of the Neolithic sites of southern China is obscure, and many must come far into the Bronze Age. Per-haps those of the Huai river basin are as old as the end of the Neolithic period in the Central Plain, where the Lung Shan culture was superseded by the Shang bronze culture in the seventeenth or sixteenth century B.C. One regional group of sites spread around the south-east coast from Chekiang to Kuantung is demonstrably later than the southern outliers of the Lung Shan culture with which it overlaps in the river valleys around Hangchou Bay on the Chekiang coast. The uniformity of pottery and stone tools found on more than a hundred of these sites justifies the recognition of a distinct South-East Neolithic culture. Like their contemporaries in the Yangtze valley, the Neolithic population of the south-eastern provinces are mound-dwellers. Their habitations occupied low hillocks on river terraces or by the sea shore, often in groups. Their remains are specially abundant on the lower courses of rivers flowing to the coast in Fukien province, and scores of their habitation sites have been traced at Hongkong and on the adjacent islands. The largest of the sites recently excavated is at T'an Shih Shan near Foochow. The mound is some 500 metres long, 10 metres wide and raised between 10 and 20 metres above the general ground level. Much of the mound consists of sea shells gathered for food—as in the northern fringe-areas of the European Neolithic, hunting had been reduced to its lowest form. The axes, adzes and arrowheads of polished stone resemble the Yangtze types, but the pottery is distinct and much superior. Much of it is of a thin brownish ware baked to a hardness which argues the possession of a kiln capable of temperatures of at least 1000 degrees centigrade. It is decorated with repeated stamped patterns of squared spirals, hachuring, and impressions of cords, matting and shells. Some fragments are covered with a red clay slip and others painted in black with simple geometric motifs. The potter's wheels and moulds were used, though the majority of the ware is hand-made. Stone spindle-whorls are proof of weaving. Agriculture is attested here only by large polished stones which can only have served as hoes, but at other related sites the crescentic stone reaping-knife has been found.

In Chekiang deposits the hard stamped ware has been discovered overlying Lung Shan pottery. Here the South-Eastern Neolithic is evidently contemporary with the Bronze culture of the Central Plain. It is suspected of surviving well into the last millennium B.C. At a Hongkong site its characteristic pottery occurred together with a bronze halberd of a type current in the eighth–seventh centuries B.C. Such peripheral and belated communities had no contribution to make to the advance of Chinese civilisation. Cultural progress was inseparably linked with the destinies of the Central Plain, to an account of whose Bronze Age lords we now turn.

CHAPTER II

The Earlier Bronze Age: the Shang Dynasty

IN COMPARISON WITH the slower development seen in the Near East and Europe, the transition in central China from a Neolithic to an advanced Bronze Age culture is mysteriously abrupt. In the course of a few centuries the villages of the plain fell under the domination of walled cities on whose rulers the possession of bronze weapons, chariots and slaves conferred a measure of superiority to which no Neolithic community could aspire, however populous and well fed. The event took place about the middle of the second millennium B.C. Not much earlier the Neolithic tribesmen of Europe, Britain and Scandinavia had become acquainted with bronze and come under civilising influences which can be traced ultimately to the Mediterranean and the Middle East. At about the same time Bronze Age culture spread eastwards through Asia and beyond the Urals. It was tempting to connect the rise of the Shang civilisation of China with similar influences of Western origin. But if it is to be a cultural migration comparable to those which radiated in the West from the Near East, there remains an awkward gap—which Loehr has tried to fill by postulating the existence of a 'Northern Culture', as yet undefined, which might supply the missing link in the chain of events in central China.

One reason for suggesting that a fully formed bronze-using culture migrated thence from the West lies in the absence in China of a truly primitive stage of bronze metallurgy. In the Early Bronze Age of Western Asia and Europe, open moulds were used to cast simple flat axes and daggers and a few ornamental pins and plaques. In China the earliest bronze products so far unearthed attest a much more advanced technique of casting. One purpose for which the Chinese seem to have

employed the metal from the start—the manufacture of orna/
mented ritual vessels—indicates a greater accumulation of
wealth in the hands of a few than does the more limited enter/
prise of the earliest bronze/users in the West. It is improbable
that evidence for a truly primitive level of bronze metallurgy in
central China can have been overlooked in the archaeological
research of the last thirty years. On the other hand, neither the
forms of bronze vessels and weapons nor the written record of
Shang and Chou history supports the theory of a large trans/
ference of people or culture from the far West.

In these circumstances we must conclude that little beyond a
knowledge of the metallurgical technique reached China from
outside, and that this borrowing was not accompanied by social
and artistic influences which would justify us in speaking
of a transfer of culture. The rapid mastery of the bronze
technique in Shang times and its application to the manufacture
of objects and ornament of purely Chinese invention is no
more surprising than the rapid adoption of bronze by more
primitive communities as the civilisation of central China ex/
panded southwards. There too bronze was used from the start
to produce weapons and vessels of advanced design and
sophisticated ornament.

THE
CHRONOLOGY
OF SHANG
SITES
The continuity between the Shang Bronze Age and the
Lung Shan Neolithic tradition in the Central Plain has
been demonstrated on a score of sites. In almost every con/
siderable excavation in Honan the grey pottery of Shang lies
directly over layers containing the black Lung Shan ware.
This was true of the most important Shang site which has
been investigated, the royal capital at Hsiao T'un near Anyang[1]
in the north of Honan. Large/scale excavations were carried
out here from 1929 to 1937. Attention had been attracted to it in
1902, when a search for the source of the 'dragon/bones' which
were being ground up by apothecaries as a medicine led to the
fields outside Hsiao T'un. Earlier Lo Chen/yü had recog/

nised that the inscriptions present on many of the 'dragon-bones' were oracle texts of great antiquity, and in the vicinity of Hsiao T'un, it was noted, an ancient tradition located the site of Yin Hsü, the 'Waste of Yin' mentioned in the histories. Yin was an alternative name for the house of Shang apparently used by their Chou successors, and the waste remained when the latter conquered the Shang and transferred the capital elsewhere. The discoveries made at Hsiao T'un were dramatic. The inscribed bones, which proved to record oracular texts, established beyond doubt that this was the capital of the later kings of the Shang. These remains are not, however, the earliest which are attributed to the Shang period.[2]

Since 1953 numerous Shang sites have been investigated close to the city of Cheng Chou, in Honan province, about 160 km. south of Anyang. They have thrown light on Shang culture as it existed before the foundation of the capital at Hsiao T'un and provide the first satisfactory evidence for a chronological sequence within the Shang period. The following scheme summarises conclusions reached by a comparison of the two main Shang sites excavated thus far:

c. 1500 to *c.* 1300 B.C.	SHANG I	(Early Period) cf. Cheng Chou, Lo Ta Miao, Tung Chai I
	SHANG II	(Early Middle Period) cf. Cheng Chou, Erh Li Kang I
	SHANG III	(Late Middle Period) cf. Cheng Chou, Erh Li Kang II
c. 1300 to *c.* 1150 B.C.	SHANG IV	(Late Period, Early Hsiao T'un) cf. Cheng Chou People's Park; Hsiao T'un below rammed-earth foundations
c. 1150 to *c.* 1027 B.C.	SHANG V	(Late Period, Late Hsiao T'un) cf. Hsiao T'un, period of rammed-earth foundations.[3]

The scale of the fortifications found at Cheng Chou, and attributed to the second earliest phase of the site, imply a city of even larger size than Great Shang at Hsiao T'un. This may have been Hsiao,[4] whither history reports the tenth Shang king (Chung Ting) to have moved his capital from a location farther east. The district comprised within a radius of 15 km. around Cheng Chou appears to have been no less densely inhabited from the Neolithic period onwards than was the territory surrounding the capital at Hsiao T'un. Near Cheng Chou many habitation sites of Yang Shao and Lung Shan type have been discovered, mostly occupying low hillocks which raised them a few feet above the general level of the flood plain of the river. The site held to be the earliest Shang Bronze Age settlement, near the village of Lo Ta Miao, is on a piece of rising ground some 15 km. to the west of Cheng Chou. The habitation layer connected with a vertical-sided pit 3 metres deep. Nearby a child was buried with a stone axe, and another grave contained a pottery tripod vessel.

The pottery kilns at Lo Ta Miao are a variant of the Neolithic type known from Pan P'o Ts'un. A roughly circular pit, about a yard in diameter is provided with a stoking-hole at the side and capped by a clay cover pierced by four or five flues. The grey pottery baked in these kilns is, however, distinct from that of the Yang Shao tradition, in the fabric resembling more closely the pottery of later Shang times, and among its shapes including some which connect with the Lung Shang tradition.

A similar pottery was found at the site of Tung Chai, under a layer corresponding to the lower level at the larger site of Erh Li Kang, another hillock settlement lying 1 km. south of Cheng Chou. At Erh Li Kang two successive levels, designated here Shang II and III, were clearly defined; and at the People's Park site at the north-west corner of the city a layer corresponding by its contents to the upper level of Erh Li Kang was obtruded on by pits and house floors which justify the recognition of a further stage, Shang IV. This admittedly limited and scattered stratigraphical evidence is reinforced by the logical development of pottery shapes through the series of sites, by the changing forms of decorated bone pins and the increasing refinement of the technique of oracle-taking (see p. 99).

At Hsiao T'un the most striking stratigraphical feature is the appearance of large building foundations of rammed earth, or pisé, such as could only be built by a large and disciplined labour force. The foundations are taken as the criterion for dividing the duration of the city into earlier and later phases, Shang IV and V in the table. The latest pottery forms found at Cheng Chou are claimed by the excavators to resemble those occurring at Hsiao T'un beneath the level of the building foundations. The latest phase identified at Cheng Chou would thus correspond to the earlier occupation of the northern city. Unfortunately the success of the excavations at Cheng Chou in defining the earlier Shang deposits has not been repeated at Hsiao T'un. While recognising the level of rammed earth foundations as an important stratigraphical feature, Li Chi and his collaborators in the pre-war excavations in general despaired of reducing the complicated pits, graves and channels of the site to a simple stratigraphical order.[5]

Whether a metal-less Neolithic economy of Lung Shan tradition persisted around Hsiao T'un until the Shang kings made it their capital (as the stratigraphy at some sites might suggest) is still uncertain. Conversely, the history of the Shang city at Cheng Chou after the establishment of the capital at Hsiao T'un remains quite obscure. Possibly the material which would clarify this question lies buried under the modern city.

The wide scatter of the earlier sites around Cheng Chou reflects a village economy. An earthen city wall, the mark of the urbanisation characteristic of the polity and economic life of a Bronze Age city-state, seems to have been built as early as

Fig. 24

WALLS
AND
BUILDINGS

Shang II, i.e. probably in the fifteenth century B.C. The trace of the foundation of the wall, 19–20 metres wide and built of layers of rammed earth 7–10 cm. thick, has been followed for 1720 metres west from the site of Paio Chia Chuang. At either end of this line its south-running extensions soon connect with the existing ancient city wall of Cheng Chou, with lengths of 2000 and 1725 metres in west and east respectively. In the fabric of the ancient wall fragments of Lung Shan and Shang I pottery were found, and on top of it habitation material and burials attributed to Shang III. Beneath the southern line of the existing wall ancient rammed-earth foundations were also found, but their attribution to Shang II or III remains doubtful. Evidently the Shang wall was intended to be a square of some 1920 metres' side. The square plan and its orientation were to be followed by Chinese city walls in later times. Thus far, strange as its absence appears, no city wall has been traced at Hsiao T'un.[6]

The same method of construction as used for the wall, the compacting of successive thin layers of soil by ramming with narrow staves (ram marks of 5 cm. diameter were distinguishable in the wall), was followed to prepare the foundations of buildings. The earliest house floor was excavated at Paio Chia Chuang. It was cut into by another house floor dated to Shang III, and is therefore assigned to Shang II, the period which saw the city wall raised. The earth platform destined to carry the building measured 25·5 by 8·8 metres. Foundations of this type are rare at Cheng Chou, perhaps because they were reserved for important buildings or the houses of the wealthy, as the expense of labour it required might suggest. When two or three centuries later they appear at Hsiao T'un more commonly, these foundations are sometimes on a grand scale and preserve features which give an idea of the form of building they supported. In the important sector C, a complex of rectangular foundations is related to surrounding ritual burials in a way

Fig. 11

which suggests that the buildings they supported existed con⁄temporaneously and were built to a general plan. The scale of the foundations and the rites which accompanied their con⁄struction seem appropriate to palaces or temples. The plat⁄forms are of rammed earth, averaging 2 metres in depth, partly sunk beneath the contemporary ground level. The largest is that lying to the north, which was 25 metres wide, and of greater though uncertain length. In the south of the sector narrower buildings formed three sides of a hollow square open to the east. Here and there river boulders had been placed on the sur⁄face of the platforms as footings of pillars, which were of wood. At another part of the Hsiao T'un site a rectangular foundation 30 metres long preserved regular alignments of such boulders. The pillars on the perimeter stood about 4 metres apart. The space of about 7 metres across the width of the building was divided by a central row of pillars.

In these dimensions we detect the first appearance of the trabeate wooden architecture of the Chinese type as it has sur⁄vived to modern times in China, Korea and Japan. The spaces are those which could be easily bridged by timbers, and the approximately equal spacing of the bays in both axes of the foundations foreshadows a lasting feature of the wooden archi⁄tecture. A single bronze pillar⁄footing was recovered, in the form of a disc measuring 35 cm. in diameter and made convex on the underside so as to rest on a boulder, but the use of bronze for this purpose was exceptional. Large boulders were (and still are) the usual means of firming the foot of a pillar and preventing its decay. Little can be said of the roofing and walls of these buildings. No trace of tiles is reported by the excavators, so we may assume that the covering was of wood, thatch or daub, and the absence of any form of bricks suggests that already in Shang times builders closed the spaces between the pillars with the same light partitions as have been used in the traditional architecture until the present day.

Chinese archaeologists accept the rammed-earth (pisé) method of building as characteristic of the Bronze Age; ordinary dwelling-houses of the Shang period were, however, raised on earth floors without the compacted foundation, and often on a floor lowered below the level of the surrounding ground in the same way as in Neolithic times. From Hsiao T'un round 'pit-dwellings' are described, most of which are about 2 metres deep and 3 to 5 metres in diameter, often with traces of an earth wall around the lip. But the sunken houses of Shang II at Cheng Chou a century or two earlier, are less primitive. An irregular row of rectangular foundations was uncovered at the site of Ming Kung Lu in the north-west of the city, roughly aligned with their longer axes parallel. This arrangement hints at the checker-board pattern, already implied in the square wall of the Shang city, which was to be the basis of later Chinese town planning. The houses measured on average 3 by 1·5 metres and were mostly sunk half a metre below the old ground surface. Their doors were on a long side and fireplaces were made at the wall near them. Some had round or square niches

KEY TO OPPOSITE PAGE

1	Dog	14	Find of *ko* halberd etc.
2	Caprid	15	Find of a *chüeh* etc.
3	Pig	16	Find of a *ting* etc.
4	Bovid	17	Bird
5	Horse	18	Burial of a person upside-down (on head)
6	Chariot		
7	Child	19	Kneeling victim holding shield and halberd (*ko*)
8	Woman		
9	Kneeling man	20	Kneeling victim holding halberd (*ko*)
10	Stone pillar-footing		
11	Find of ritual vessels	21	Rammed earth foundation
12	Grave of beheaded sacrificial victims	22	Stone pillar-footing resting on a mound of rammed earth
13	Find of a *lei*		

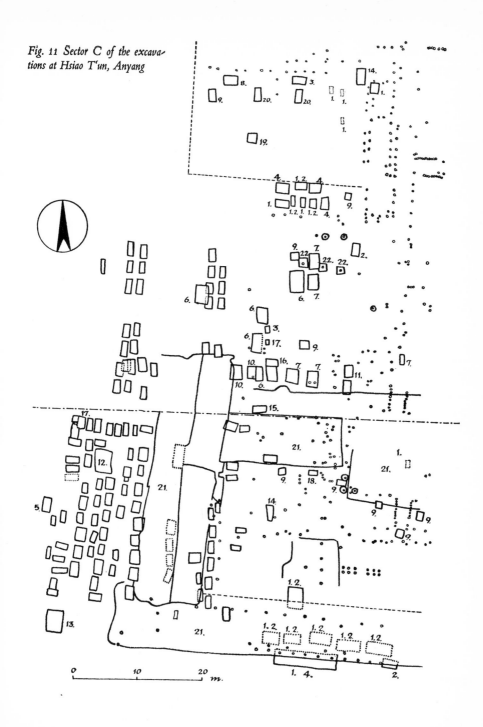

Fig. 11 Sector C of the excavations at Hsiao T'un, Anyang

hollowed in the wall, which had possibly served as stoves, and recall the internal arrangements of the huts at the Neolithic village of Pan Po. In the Shang III stage the houses were often treated in the original and hygienic fashion already known in the Lung Shan Neolithic, the floors and the internal footings of the walls being thickly coated with lime wash. The plans are rectangular, generally undivided as before, and laid either on the ground level or sunk below it only a little. One such house at Ming Kung Lu, which overlay the foundations of some of those just described, was considerably bigger than its predecessors, measuring 16 by 7.5 metres. Five small storage pits inside had received the same coating of lime as the floor and lower walls. At Tzŭ Ching a number of similar houses were aligned at intervals of about ten metres, each measuring about 3 by 7 metres. One floor consisted of two layers of thick lime separated by a layer of soil. The walls were of compacted earth, up to a metre in thickness, and one house was divided by a central wall. The doors were on the long side, with the fireplace near-by. There is no sign in the Shang house-plans we have described of the courtyard house which existed in the Han period and remained the traditional domestic design in China ever after.

Beyond the arrangement implied in the rectangular plan and in some cases the alignment of the houses, the information we have at present helps little in visualising the appearance of a Shang city. But if the rectangular city plan had already been adopted, we perhaps may surmise something of the layout from the later practice. According to the Chou Li, a ritual work of the third or second century B.C., the proper design for a city in the Chou period was held to be the square or rectangle, with the sides orientated to the four cardinal directions. This was the plan of the T'ang capital of Ch'ang An, and of the Japanese imperial capitals which copied it, and it is repeated in the existing palace precincts of Peking. In this scheme the palace or an equivalent large building stands near the centre and faces south along a broad street leading to the south gate. Around this nucleus streets were laid in checker-board pattern. For a capital city this design later had a ritual significance, the south-facing aspect of the palace, and hence of the ruler enthroned, being essential to the proper exercise of imperial power. We need not suppose that in early times the area enclosed by the wall was fully occupied by buildings. The political role of the city as dominating an ill-defined region beyond its walls would require it to serve on occasion as a refuge for the peasants who looked to it for protection. Within its walls great buildings might still stand amid fields and plantations. A rectangular pattern of broad streets leading to a central citadel would be as fitting a design for military purposes as was the somewhat similar plan of a Roman camp.

The deep pits found in and near Shang habitations are similar to those of Neolithic times and like them are presumed to have served for storing grain. Often they were carefully shaped. One excavated at Liu Li Ko near Hui Hsien in Honan province was 11 metres deep. Its vertical profile is characteristic of the Shang pits. From an oval mouth, measuring some 2 by 3 metres, it narrows about half-way down to a neat rectangular plan of 1 by 2 metres. Pits 4–5 metres in depth were found at Erh Li Kang, where two pits contained human skeletons in crouched and prone positions, apparently casual burials. These examples are attributed to the Shang III period. At Hsiao T'un the pits were ubiquitous; in a season's work 127 of them were excavated in two sectors. Narrow rectangular shafts went to depths of 4–5 metres, but many were shallower, several metres in diameter, and provided with earth-cut steps descending along the wall. From one such pit were recovered the seven tortoise carapaces, intact and inscribed, from which the methods of the augurs were first deduced. The contents of the inscribed sentences indicate oracles taken in the time of the

STORAGE
PITS

Fig. 12

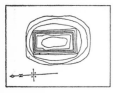

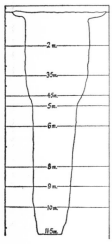

Fig. 12 Plan and vertical section of a storage pit at Hui Hsien: Shang period

twenty-sixth Shang king, towards the middle of the Shang occupation of the site. All seven shells bore the name of the same augur, and they appeared to have been filed as archives and deliberately stored below ground. Another shaft-like pit, 1·8 metres wide and some 6 metres deep, produced 17,906 pieces of oracular bone and tortoise-shell, including more than 300 intact carapaces. The majority of them had been used in augury and a large proportion of them were inscribed. This material lay in a compact mass in the middle region of the pit, occupying a depth of 1·6 metres, and sloping from one side as if it had been tipped in from the mouth. Below the bones were some 3 metres of the greenish filling which the excavators believed to represent decayed vegetable matter, while above lay the grey soil common to all the habitation levels of the site. Here we seem to have a refuse dump rather than a subterranean library.

A problem not yet satisfactorily solved is that of the latest date of the Shang occupation of the Hsiao T'un site. The Shang floors are found only a metre or two below the modern surface, which in the opinion of the excavators shows signs of having been scoured by the flooding of the Huan River. This may have destroyed signs of habitation extending into the Chou period. But since no Chou material has been identified in the tombs on the site (which being deeper buried would escape the effects of flooding), it seems improbable that the life of the city continued for long after the fall of the Shang dynasty. History recounts that a brother of the last Shang king received back the capital as his fief, to be held under Chou suzerainty. The archaeological evidence shows that the importance of the city declined suddenly upon the advent of Chou rule, even if it was not totally abandoned until some generations had passed.

Apart from the oracle texts, and the traces of potters' shops and bone and bronze workshops, the finds made in Shang storage pits and house foundations have not been spectacular.

The contents of the graves are more impressive. Some vast pit-tombs in the vicinity of Hsiao T'un which are attributed to the later period of the site (Shang V), can be none other than the burials of Shang kings. Their excavation revealed not only some striking examples of Shang art but some of the grimmest holocausts ever perpetrated by Bronze Age despots.

The royal cemetery at Hsi Pei Kang, a piece of low rising ground near the village of Hou Chia Chuang, lies beyond the Huan River 3 km. north-west of Hsiao T'un. The tombs are not marked by any overground structures, and only barely perceptible depressions indicated their position. Eight tombs, seven of cruciform plan and one square, are set close together, with occasional overlapping of their outer edges. The cruciform tombs consist of a deep central shaft with almost vertical sides, from the four sides of which ramps ascend to the surface. In each case the southern ramp is the principal approach to the burial chamber, and the orientation is uniform, the northern ramp pointing in a direction 14–15 degrees east of north. The structure of the burial chambers, which were built of close-set squared timbers (now perished but traceable in soil impressions) is that followed in great tombs until the end of the Chou period. An outer chamber enclosed a much smaller coffin which lay on its floor at the centre and covered a small rectangular sacrificial pit. In the earth filling which intervened between the coffin and the outer wooden walls, on the surface of the pit bottom which continued the level of the roof of the outer burial chamber, and on the floors of the ramps, were laid the grave-gifts of pottery and bronze vessels, bronze weapons, ornaments, stone figures, carved bone and ivory, jades and the remains of victims, human and animal, slaughtered to make a king's funeral.

The funeral procession entered the tomb from the south, for the southern ramps led to the floor of the burial chamber itself, while the other three, mostly stepped, led to the broad

THE GREAT
SHANG TOMBS

Fig. 13

Plate 8

shelf level with its roof. In Tomb 1001 the chamber is cruci⸗
form, its top 6 metres underground and its depth 4 metres.
Allowing for the step, each arm of the cruciform bottom of the
pit measured about 20 metres. The ramps extended some 15
metres east and west and some 20 metres north and south.
The other tombs vary slightly in their dimensions, the largest
of them having a surface plan totalling 1200 square metres,
and their burial chambers were square. The northward turn
of the end of the western ramp of Tomb 1217 and the steps

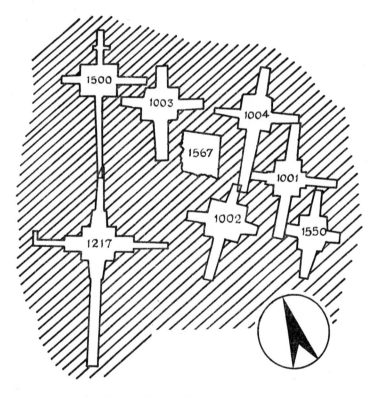

*Fig. 13 Plan of group of great tombs at Hsi Pei Kang, near Anyang.
Late Shang period*

leading from the side to the bottom of the northern ramp of Tomb 1500 are exceptional features. Burials of human victims were traced in three of the tombs. Twice a man was found buried with a dog in the basal sacrificial pit underneath the coffin (1001 and 1550), and in the same tombs human victims were buried at the four corners of the burial chamber, in the former in a kneeling posture and with mouths wide open. A heap of human skulls was found on one of the ramps of Tomb 1500, and on the steps of the northern ramp of Tomb 1550 human skulls were neatly arranged in rows of ten. The tomb with approximately square surface plan (1567) is described as a false tomb, for it descended to a depth of only 4·3 metres. Nevertheless it contained traces of a central wooden burial chamber, and some carved stone and bone objects and bronze vessels.

Inside the burial chambers of the royal tombs hardly anything was found, for they had all been plundered, in ancient and recent times. From them came no doubt many of the splendid bronzes which dealers purveyed to museums and private collections in the first decades of the present century. But the finds made in the approach ramps and on the step near the burial chambers included some of the finest examples of Shang art.[7] In Tomb 1004, at the juncture of the southern ramp with the burial chamber lay two four-legged bronze vessels of the *ting* type, measuring 74 and 63 cm. to the rim. The chief decoration of the sides of the first is a bull mask, and of the other a deer mask, and they are inscribed respectively as 'bull *ting*' and 'deer *ting*', perhaps in allusion to the sacrificial animals to which they were appropriated. Near-by lay a set of three musical stones. The carved limestone figures which had been placed on the ramps introduce us to a branch of Shang art which had not been revealed among the finds made on the habitation sites. In nearly all of the royal tombs the upper surface of the roof of the burial chamber preserved the remains of some

Plate 7

kind of canopy which had covered it at the time of the funeral. The fabric was wood, surviving in the form of earth impressions retaining the paint and inlays which decorated it. The chief colour was red, with yellow, black and white. Limestone, mother-of-pearl, ivory and turquoise contributed to the inlay, and in one instance gold foil. The subjects depicted were dragons, tigers, birds, the conventionalised animal mask later to be called *t'ao t'ieh*, and the continuous spiral design called thunder pattern from its resemblance to a Shang ideograph. The west ramp of Tomb 1217 revealed, preserved in the same fugitive fashion, the trace of a large wooden drum covered with 'snake-skin'. A unique bronze in the Sumitomo collection in Kyoto, Japan, is a metal version of a similar drum.

The solemn burial of kings attested by the rich grave-goods and the dedication of human and animal victims in the cruci-form tombs did not exhaust the sumptuous rites which accom-panied a Shang royal funeral. Some at least among the 411 smaller tombs grouped apart a short distance to the east must have been filled in the course of the royal inhumations. Here some pits contained only headless human skeletons, buried with stone axes and bronze knives, while others held only rows of severed heads, ten at a time. One pit was filled with the dismantled parts of a chariot. Horses with head rope and bronze ornaments were buried apart, in one instance four together; in eight other pits in pairs. Monkeys, dogs and deer were among the slaughtered animals. In a pit to itself was buried an ele-phant.

Plate 11

Fig. 22

Plate 9

Another tomb of royal dimensions may yet remain to be dis-covered near the village of Ta Ssŭ K'ung, on the north side of the Huan river, for here in 1952 was excavated an intact chariot burial, which we have reason to believe was a satellite of a king's grave. Still nearer to Hsiao T'un, on the same side of the river, the royal tomb excavated at Wu Kuan Ts'un in 1950 is of the same form as those at Hsi Pei Kang, but has ramps

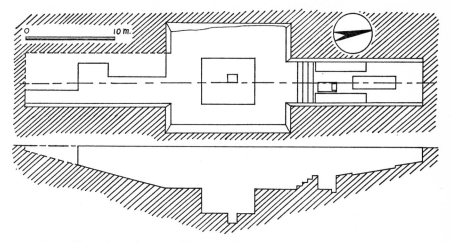

Fig. 14 Plan and vertical section of the great tomb at Wu Kuan Ts'un, near Anyang. Late Shang period

only to north and south, orientated as before. The burial chamber, however, had suffered less depredation, and from its contents we may see what objects were placed nearest to the principal occupant of a great tomb. The outer chamber had been covered by the usual painted and inlaid wooden canopy. Inside, between the wall of the chamber and the space where the inner coffin had stood, were found a scatter of shell and turquoise ornaments, a jade knife and a jade *pi* ring, stone vessels of *p'an* and *yü* forms, white pottery vessels comprising *hu, lei p'an* and *ts'un*, a vase of the thin, hard variety of pottery, and bronze vessels of the forms *ting, chia, chüeh, kuei, fang yi* and *lei*; and bone pins, bronze halberds and arrowheads. On the step lay a musical stone carved with the design of a tiger, twenty-four human victims and eleven dogs. The ramps were guarded by sentinels, one buried crouched, the other holding a halberd. Three pits in the north ramp together held sixteen slaughtered horses, and further dogs and horses were buried in the south

Fig. 14

Plate 10

ramp. In the rammed-earth filling of the pit over the burial chamber were included the bodies of deer, monkeys and dogs, and in an upper layer thirty-four human skulls set upright in rows and looking towards the centre. In small pits to the south of the main tomb were found headless human skeletons buried in groups of ten.

The tomb at Wu Kuan Ts'un village has been ascribed, on the stylistic evidence of its contents, to the earlier Hsiao T'un period, Shang IV. The overlapping of the ramps of tombs in the Hsi Pei Kang group and their large number suggests that they cover a longer period than the century and a half or so represented by one of the chronological divisions, and belong as a group to both Shang IV and Shang V. No tombs of comparable size have yet been dated to earlier times.

The smaller tombs known in Shang III and later are simple rectangular earth pits without entrance ramps, 2–3 metres long and 1–2 metres wide, sometimes with a wooden burial cham-ber sunk to the level of a step in the side of the pit. Victims in the shape of dogs, pigs and even human beings occur even in these humbler graves, and pottery and bronze vessels are placed inside the burial chamber or on the step outside. Whether or not there is a wooden burial chamber and an inner coffin, a tomb of any pretensions will be furnished with the basal sacrificial pit holding an animal victim. The body of the chief occupant, like those of the human victims in the great tombs, may be laid prone or supine.

The sacrifice of human and animal victims was not confined to the occasion of royal funerals. The excavations in sector C which revealed the building foundations of palaces and temples produced evidence of a vast slaughter clearly connected with the consecration and the spiritual guardianship of the buildings, much of it, one must assume, performed in a single rite. Sacrificial pits were dug around the edge of the foundations of the principal buildings. In front of the east–west building in the

Plate 12

Fig. 11

north the pits held cows, goats, and dogs. On the east side of the long north–south building were buried chiefly groups of headless human skeletons. Outside and either side of gate–ways (the position of these being inferred from alignments of the boulders serving as pillar footings) were buried kneeling men and women, the former armed with halberds and some holding shields, all facing south. Below the pisé foundations cows and goats were buried, and within the pisé, dogs, singly and in groups of five. In the space which must have formed a court enclosed by the buildings, besides men holding weapons and bronze vessels, five chariots had been buried. Four of these burials had been disturbed, but one intact pit contained the dis–cernible remains of the chariot's complement of four horses and three armed men.

Soon after the fall of the Shang dynasts their practice of human sacrifice seems to have been forgotten. Rare instances only are recorded from the early Chou period. Even Con–fucius seems to have been ignorant of it, for he surely, had he known, would have cited the abolition of human sacrifice upon the advent of the Chou rulers as a sign of the superior morality he claims for them. According to a remark quoted by Mencius, he deplored the practice of burying human effigies of wood with the dead, but said nothing of the less humane custom which this replaced. No trace has survived of such effigies before the third century B.C., perhaps only because wood so rarely survives in dry soil. From the Han period on–wards tomb figurines of clay are not only common but con–stitute one of the most interesting branches of Chinese art; and in the T'ang period their variety and aesthetic quality make them comparable to the terracottas of ancient Greece.

In the Shang as in the Neolithic period the commonest form of grave–goods are vessels, now made of bronze as well as pot–tery. The bronzes show the greater variety of types, their shapes and their grouping as libation or drinking vessels (*chüeh* and

THE RITUAL
BRONZE
VESSELS

ku) or vessels for preparing sacrificial meats (*li*, *ting*, *hsien*) and wine jars (*tsun*, *yü*) reflect an elaborate ritual in which food and drink were offered to spirits. Only a few bronze vessels, such as those from Erh Li Kang, can be reliably assigned to the Shang I–III. While these are comparatively simple in design and decoration, they already exploit the potentialities of metal-casting with a skill which foreshadows the superb craft of the Hsiao T'un bronze-smiths. The simpler forms, the tripod vessels *ting* and *li*, and the *kuei* bowl, have a general likeness to neolithic pottery types. Ceramic parallels whether neolithic or of the early Shang period do not, however, explain the evolution of the more elaborate and peculiar types. Once established as ritually correct the vessels continued in use for a varying length of time in the Chou period, being gradually replaced or joined by other forms. Their uses in sacrifice were eventually codified in such late-Chou texts as the Li Chi and the Chou Li. The greatest variety of shapes is found in the Shang period.

Fig. 15
Plate 21

The sacrificial meats were cooked in the *li*, *ting* and *hsien*. The first resembles the pottery *li* in having the lower part of the body divided by grooves into three lobes, though unlike the neolithic *li*, the lobes generally have short solid legs attached, and vertical handles are attached on the rim. Often each lobe is

Plate 28

decorated with the *t'ao t'ieh* mask. The *ting* has three solid, pillar-like legs, and the body is round and usually smooth.

Fig. 15e

The true *li* is comparatively rare, probably because it was chiefly made in earlier Shang times, from which fewer bronzes are known. A form intermediate between the *li* and *ting*, with the lobes less pronounced, is commoner, and survives into the

Fig. 15i

tenth century B.C. The *hsien* seems to have served as a steamer, the lower part being shaped like a *li* (in Shang pieces almost invariably decorated with bull-like masks of design distinct from the varieties of *t'ao t'ieh*) and separated from the bowl-shaped upper part by a grill. Another cooking-vessel also termed *ting* is four-legged and has a rectangular body with flat vertical sides, and the same name is given to a rare form of shallow bowl set on three legs shaped into birds or dragons.

The vessel used in the offering of the cooked meats is the *kuei*. Its simplest form (sometimes distinguished by the name *yü*) is a bowl on a ring foot with outward-sloping sides and an out-turned lip. This shape is rarely found after the close of the Shang period. The commoner form of *kuei*, squat of body with slightly bulging sides and furnished with two ring-handles set below the lip, appears to have been made at Hsiao T'un only

Fig. 15k, l

a   b   c   d

e   f   g   h

i   j   k   l

Fig. 15 *Ritual bronze vessels of the Shang period: a,* chüeh; *b,* chih; *c.* tsün; *d ,*ting; *e,* li; *f,* yü; *g,* tsun; *h,* lei; *i,* hsien; *j,* p'an; *k,* kuei; *l,* kuei. *Scale approx. 1:8*

towards the end of the Shang period. Since with the advent of the Chou it became the commonest of the ritual food-vessels, it is possible that its appearance there marks an in-fluence from the Chou homeland farther west.

The gods were attracted to the sacrifice by wine no less than by cooked meats. At least four vessel forms seem to have held *Fig. 15c, g, b* the 'black wine' mentioned in the ritual texts. The *lei* is a tall, shouldered vase with flaring lip, the *tsun* a vase of more cylin-*Plates 14, 15* drical form, generally with a rounded bulge at the centre, or with a profile sagging in an S-curve. Both forms of *tsun* are *Plate 18* related to libation goblets, the former to the slender *ku*, and the latter to the *chih*. The constriction at the middle of the *ku* *Fig. 15b* coincides with the bottom of the container. In profile it is in-variably marked by a thickening which together with the ex-panding upper and lower parts divides the ornament into three distinct panels. In many pieces two or four cross-shaped holes are pierced in the side just below the middle, for what purpose it is not known. Here there can be no question of a ceramic prototype, and it has been plausibly suggested that the shape originated in a goblet made of two horns joined together.

Plate 19 Two bucket-shaped vessels, the *yu* with lid and swinging *Fig. 15f* handle and the *hu* with vertical tubes near the lip intended for a rope-handle, are also wine-containers. The wine could be *Plate 17* poured in the spouted *ho*; the strange *kuang*, shaped like a sauce-*Plate 29* boat with lid formed into an ox-like monster and often other plastic decoration of fantastic animals, is said to have been used for mixing it. Some *kuang* have a vertical partition inside and are accompanied by a ladle. Vessels cast in the form of entire animals (owl, tiger, elephant and rhinoceros are found) prob-*Plates 20, 23* ably also held the ritual drink. The strange *chüeh* and *chia*, which also belong to the group of wine vessels, always have *Fig. 15a* long tapering, splayed legs, sharp-edged with triangular section, and, rising from the lip, a pair of short rectangular-sectioned *Plate 20* pillars carrying round caps at the top. Pottery versions of these goblets are found in considerable numbers, but it is clear that these copy the bronze forms rather than the reverse. The long spout of the *chüeh* would be better adapted to pouring a libation than to drinking, but the larger *chia* seems surprisingly little suited to either. The pillars beneath the caps are always left undecorated. If they were intended, as has been surmised, for gripping by tongs when the wine was heated over a fire, they must have been devised for a metal vessel in the first place. The design of these uncompromising shapes shows a fine feeling for plastic form.

The quality of the best Shang bronzes was not equalled by any other bronze-founders of like early date, and rarely surpassed at any time since. Excavation has thrown some light on the technique which was employed, though many details of the process are still obscure. Bronze factories were discovered at two sites near Cheng Chou. One, dated to Shang III, was at Tzŭ Hsing Shan and occupied part of a rectangular building resembling other house foundations. Traces of corroded bronze covered the floor, in which were sunk a dozen small conical pits with smooth hardened sides. These probably held the casting moulds, for the lips of the pits were blackened and surrounded by scraps of slag. Fragments of clay moulds for knives and halberds, some decorated, were scattered about. The crucibles were made of coarse red clay, bucket-shaped and cased in a thick jacket of clay mixed with soot. A deep deposit of slag lying outside the building showed that the ore was refined on the spot. The scale of the production in the bronze factories may be judged from the site of Nan Kuan Wai at Cheng Chou, where over a thousand fragments of clay moulds for weapons, *li, chia* and *chüeh* were recovered.

The clay moulds intended for casting vessels comprised a number of separate parts fitted together at the edges by dowels, six to a dozen of them being required for a goblet or tripod bowl. In his study of the moulds Karlbeck detected particles of metal adhering to the clay, which is usually blackened and hardened on the outside, and inferred that the process was one of direct casting, the molten bronze being poured into the original clay form. This argument appears to be conclusive, surprising as it is that the perfect, minute detail of the ornament of the bronze vessels could be produced by this means. At Hsiao T'un a bronze working-floor lay beneath one of the large foundation platforms in sector B, and is therefore dated to Shang IV, the earlier phase of the capital. Here was found part of a block of burnt clay, one side of which is carved with a *t'ao t'ieh* monster mask in relief. This can only be a positive model which was used to prepare a negative mould for receiving the metal. In spite of this evidence for direct casting it is difficult to believe that even in the earlier Hsiao T'un period the Chinese should have been ignorant of another way of casting bronze—the *cire-perdue* method. This required a model to be carved or moulded first of all in wax. The wax was encased in fine clay and baked, whereby the wax was eliminated and a cavity left to receive the metal. Such a proceeding is little likely to be detectable from the rubbish left on the foundry floor since the mould would be destroyed on removing the finished casting, and it is not surprising that technologists arguing from the excavated material more readily find evidence for direct casting than for the use of wax. Nevertheless, a close examination of the Shang bronze vessels with the more elaborate ornament leaves little doubt that the wax method was employed to produce them. Their varied and often minute relief, elaborate handles and undercut projecting parts, all flawlessly rendered, are unthinkable as a task for direct casting, or at least for such casting in part-moulds of the accuracy attainable in burnt clay. It is very likely that the wax technique, so long known in the West, was conveyed to China along with the knowledge of metallurgy itself. The crispness of the relief ornament on bronze vessels of the earlier Shang period suggests that wax was used even before the development of elaborate bronze ornament at Hsiao T'un.

In recent times copper and tin ores have been mined chiefly in the south-western provinces of Kweichou and Yunnan, both of which lay outside the control of the Shang state. It is questionable whether the Shang can have been content to depend for so essential a commodity on the minor trade practicable with primitive peoples, and we have seen that the inscriptions concerning military forays do not speak of the south-eastern region. Ores may however have been exploited near Hsiao T'un itself, for tradition locates them in its vicinity and some place-names bear this out, although no trace of them remains at the present day. A recent study identified four potential sources of copper and two of tin, within a radius of 100 km. from Hsiao T'un. By the standards found in other parts of the Bronze Age world the Chinese were quite eccentric in the composition of the alloy. The proportions of copper and tin vary within wide limits, even in goods of the same class. The analysis of the metal of a *ting* has given one part of tin to ten of copper which are the normal proportions in other parts of the world. A *chüeh* contained two parts of tin to ten of copper. A practice peculiar to China is the addition of a considerable quantity of lead to the alloy. In Shang bronze the lead may amount to six per cent, though generally it is less and may be lacking altogether. The presence of lead in the alloy would somewhat reduce the melting point and by improving the flow of the metal would tend to reduce flaws and bubbles. The lead therefore serves an intelligible purpose in casting vessels in which the perfection of intricate ornament was a great desideratum. But even in a spearhead, a real weapon, and not a ceremonial piece made for burial, the proportion of lead proved to be 15 per cent, while only a trace of tin was present. Perhaps the high cost of tin and the irregularity of the supply were the reasons for the variation of the constituents of bronze; or perhaps lead/ and tin/bearing ores were regarded as equivalent ingredients. But neither explanation is con/vincing. In Chou times, when the feudal settlement expanded the political sphere and opened up new possibilities of trade, so that the tin resources of south/west China should have been more easily available, still 10 per cent to 30 per cent of lead was commonly added to the alloy.

The chief arms of Shang times were the bow and the hal/berd. The shape of the bow, which had no imperishable parts, can be seen in some emblematic symbols cast on bronze vessels. The arc had a double curve and the upper tip is often curved strongly outwards. Its length, when it appears alongside a human figure in some of the symbols, seems to have been not less than about four feet. A bow of this shape can only have been built of a number of strips of wood, possibly combined with horn. It is the ancestor of the 'compound bow' which remained the standard type in eastern Asia as long as the bow was employed.[8] Its double curve affords a powerful thrust over a short pull, and in this respect it was ideal for shooting from the confined space of a chariot/box. As far as we can tell, the horse was not ridden in the Shang period, though this type of bow was equally suitable for shooting from the saddle, and became in later times the principal weapon of the mounted steppe no/mads. On Shang sites of all periods bone arrowheads are common, and consist of a simple point of circular or triangular section with a short tang. But even at the lower level of the Erh Li Kang site (Shang II) bronze arrowheads appear, along with bone copies of them. These are triangular in outline with flat blades offset clearly from the central spine. From mid/Shang times onwards sophisticated forms were adopted, with curving edges, long trailing barbs and sometimes pierced blades. The fact that the arrow heads are hafted by means of a spike/like tang, and were never made with a socket, suggests that the shafts were generally made of reed or bamboo.

a

b

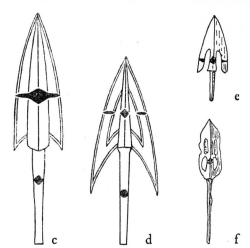

Fig. 16 a-k: Arrowheads: a, b, bone. Shang period; c, d, bronze. Shang period. From Liu Li Ko, Hui Hsien, Honan; e-g, bronze. 5th century B.C. From Chia Ko Chuang, T'ang Shan, Hopei; h-k, bronze tips of cross-bow bolts. 4th-3rd century B.C.; from Ch'eng Tu, Yang Tzŭ Shan, Szechwan. Scale 2:3

c   d   f

Fig. 18

The halberd, which in the west was never a principal arm in early times, was the chief weapon of the Shang in close fighting. It remained in use until the end of the Chou period. The Shang type commonly had a rib at the base of the blade from which projects a flat tang. The latter was inserted into a slot in a wooden haft, from which the blade projected at right angles. Rarer examples have a tubular shaft-hole, above which rises a flange—an otiose remnant of the earlier design. The appearance of the complete weapon can be surmised from the form of the character used in writing its name, *ko*, and from some of the emblematic figures. The length of the shaft appears to be about 3 feet, and it is turned up at the end beyond the blade; a decorative tassel hangs from the part of the tang which projects through the shaft, and the lower end of the shaft carries a three-pointed ferrule. Some rare examples of the latter survive.

g

h   i

Another form of Shang halberd was a long narrow blade set parallel to the shaft and generally curved a little over its end. Soldiers armed with halberds of either type carried a small shield, of which oval and rectangular forms are recorded in the

j   k

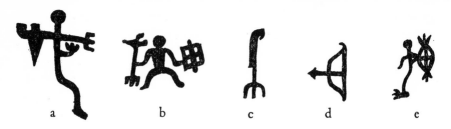

a   b   c   d   e

Fig 17 Emblematic characters cast on bronze vessels of the Shang period: a, b, e, f, l, armed men; c, g, halberds; d, h, bows; i, halberd on a shield; j, building; k, sacrificial victim; o, p, bronze ritual vessels; m, a ritual symbol of unknown meaning, possibly indicating sacrifice to ancestors; n, horsebreeder. Scale 3:4

f

script. It had apparently no imperishable parts which could survive in the tombs. A bronze helmet might be worn, though the small number of these excavated at Hsiao T'un suggests that they were not common. The helmet is a rounded cap covering the head to below the ears, a rectangular part being cut away in front to free the eyes. The ornament consists of bulging nose, eyes, eyebrows and ears cast on the dome of the helmet.

g

The script figures show also a man wielding a weapon of the same length as the *ko* but mounted with an axe blade with a broad, slightly curved edge. Many such axes have been recovered from the tombs. Most of them are decorated in low relief with monster masks—a mask with gaping fanged mouth on the blade itself and a tiger-like mask on the tang, which, like that of the halberd, is designed to pass through a slot in the shaft and to project above. Like some of the *ko*, these axes may have a round hole in the blade, and, to facilitate binding to the shaft, slots at the top of the blade and a hole in the part of the tang which the shaft would cover. Some specimens have projecting wings at the base of the blade for the same purpose. The rich cast ornament of some of the axes is hardly inferior to that of the finest bronze vessels; the same *t'ao t'ieh* masks and

h

geometric motifs are used. In some splendid pieces the designs Plates 13, 22
are formed of low cast cloisons, about one-eighth of an inch
deep, holding inlay of fragments of turquoise. The stones
rarely measure more than an eighth of an inch across, and their
edges are neatly set together and shaped to fit against the retaining walls.

In the emblematic figures cast on bronzes an axe of the type
we have described is seen held over the severed neck of a
human victim. The ornate axes with their terrifying monster
mask evidently served for the funeral slaughter, and were
thereafter consigned to the tomb. Another ceremonial tool was
a chopping-knife resembling the elongated type of halberd
blade, but provided with a handle, and designed to be used
without hafting. These too sometimes have appropriate ornament, such as the row of rams' heads—an allusion to a sacrificial animal—which decorates the upper edge of one such
knife in the British Museum.

The forms of weapons and axes we have described thus far
are without parallels in other Bronze Age centres of Asia.
But another group hints at contact, though not close or continued contact, with peoples living far to the west. China
adopted from abroad the bag-shaped axe or adze termed by
Western archaeologists socketed axe, which was the type-fossil
and an important tool of the Late Bronze Age in Europe. The
Bronze Age Karasuk culture of the Minusinsk region of
southern Siberia was an intermediary in the migration of this

m   n   o   p

Fig. 20 tool. Characteristically, the Shang socketed axes have an individual stamp, their neat rectangular form with sharply squared section differing from the more rounded shapes of the Siberian product. Some features of the metal surface suggest that the socketed axe or adze was cast in a one-piece open mould. The edge of the socket is generally decorated, on one

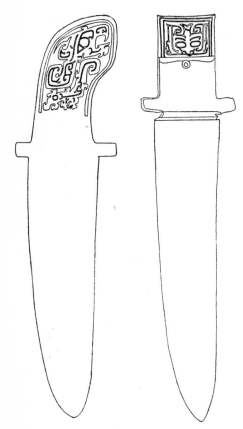

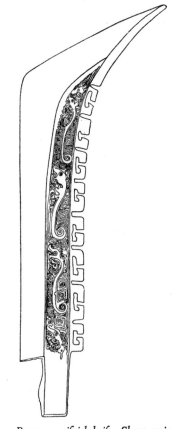

Fig. 18 Bronze halberds, ko, Shang period. Length (left) 20·5 cm. (right) 29·5 cm.

Fig. 19 Bronze sacrificial knife. Shang period. From Liu Li Ko, Hui Hsien, Honan. Length 41·5 cm.

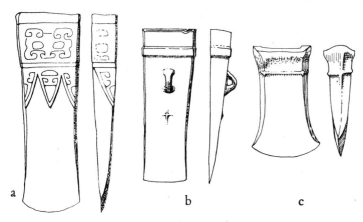

Fig. 20 *Bronze socketed axes: a, Shang period; b,
c, 10th-7th centuries B.C. Scale 5:11*

side only, with an animal mask in the usual low linear relief. One axe so decorated was found in the royal tomb at Wu Kuan Ts'un, though on the whole it appears that the socketed axes were seldom added to the grave-goods, any more than the chisels and saws whose existence we may surmise although no specimens have come down to us from Shang times.

Another form owed to the West is the spear head. It has an elegant, leaf-shaped blade and a tubular socket on which are set two ring-lugs to help the hafting. Here too the Shang armourers produced their eccentric variant of a universal Bronze Age type: the edges of the blade were continued down the sides of the socket, to end with two hafting holes just above the mouth of the socket. Spears seem not to have been made in the Karasuk period in southern Siberia, and we must imagine that the form reached China from farther afield and by a different route. At Tomsk, farther north and west in Siberia, a mould was found associating forms of socketed axe and spear which can be regarded as ancestors of the Chinese specimens.[9] The antiquity of both these types in southern Russia and the

Fig. 21b, c

Kuban district of the Caucasus is sufficient to allow their arrival as a borrowing in the Shang culture of the thirteenth to eleventh centuries B.C. But some closer analogies link directly with Minusinsk and its Karasuk culture. A few Shang axes have narrow parallel-sided blades, springing from a shafting tube, which come close to a Karasuk form.

Still more striking are a number of knives excavated at Hsiao T'un (where they seemed to be connected particularly with chariot burials) which repeat a Karasuk idea. The finish and ornament of these knives fall out of the context of the other products of the Shang foundries. The heads of horses and ibexes that decorate the ends of the handles are nearer to the more naturalistic art of southern Siberia than to the usual Chinese convention. In this instance we cannot doubt the evidence of a direct contact of the Chinese and the inhabitants of Minusinsk. We may guess from the disappearance of these knives and the animal ornament associated with them at the end of the Shang period that this contact was less effective in the early Chou period. Conversely, the Karasuk graves of southern Siberia show an increase of Mongoloid skulls in comparison with the earlier graves and so possibly indicate an ethnic move-ment thither from northern China or Mongolia. Unfortunately, since the Karasuk graves are dated only broadly to the period from 1200 to 800 B.C., it is not possible to connect this evi-dence of migration more closely with events in China, in spite of the temptation to see in this migration a result of the unrest caused by the war of Chou and Shang.

Fig. 21a Bronze knife with ram's head pommel. Late Shang period. British Museum. Scale 1:2

Plate 11

In the later part of their reign at least, the heavy arm of the Shang kings was the chariot. The excavators of Academia Sinica working in 1953 near the village of Ta Ssŭ K'ung, a few miles to the south-east of Hsia T'un, were more fortunate than the excavators of sector C (see p. 62 above) in finding an indisturbed chariot-pit whose contents were as well pre-served as any dating from Shang times. The photograph and diagram show the remains lying *in situ*. The chariot was buried intact, channels being lowered beneath the general floor level of the pit to accommodate the wheels and the main members of the frame. The structure of the wooden parts was preserved in the traces of finer, compact earth which had re⁄ placed the wood as it decayed. The only bronze parts of the carriage are the two axle caps and the sheathing of the two Λ⁄ shaped members of the yoke which rested on the horses' heads behind the ears. Lines of convex bronze discs which were attached to the bridle and the reins, and such things as a small bronze bell, bronze cheek⁄pieces and ornaments from the horses' foreheads give some idea of the harness, but much is left to conjecture.

b

The armament of the charioteer may be seen in the list which accompanies Fig. 22. The stock of arrows, tipped with bone or bronze, vouches for the bow of which no trace survived. Near the charioteer's box lay a stone blade and a knife of the Siberian kind, and two strangely shaped ob⁄ jects which have defied satisfactory explanation. Chinese archaeologists first called them 'ornaments for the bow', but have now changed the name to 'bow⁄shaped ornaments'. A fair number of such objects has reached collections. The pro⁄ jection of the terminals (these are hollow, and sometimes con⁄ tain stones to make rattles of them) below the curve of the centre portion makes the object quite unsuitable for mounting on a bow. Another suggestion is that these bronzes were attached to the edge of the driver's box as a rest for the reins: but the lack of any rivets or loops on the underside make it difficult to see how they could be attached firmly enough for this purpose. They may, to make another guess, have been mounted on shields, as an ornament and a jingle to sound when the shield was flourished. It is clear at least that these objects were not a part of the chariot itself, for one of them was found in Minusinsk, where there is no sign of chariots at all.

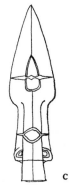

c

*Fig. 21 b, c,
Bronze spearheads.
Late Shang period.
Scale approx. 1:5*

KEY TO FIGURE 22

I Human skeleton

II, III Skeletons of horses

   IV Trace of timber of the shaft

   V Trench made to receive the shaft

   VI Trenches made to receive the wheels

VII Trace of timber of the axle

VIII Trench cut to receive the axle

   IX Trace of lower timbers of the box

   X Traces of red lacquer paint

XI Black ashy soil

1 Bronze bell
2 Gold foil
3 Cowrie shells
4 Bronze plaque
5 Bow-shaped object of bronze
6 Stone blade
7 Bronze arrowheads
8–10 Bone tubes
11 Bone arrowheads
12 Socket of a bronze axe
13 Bronze chisel
14–15 Bronze arrowheads
16 Bronze knife
17 Stone point
18 Bone tube
19 Domed disk of mother-of-pearl
20 Bone tube
21 Disk of mother-of-pearl
22 Fragments of stone point
23 Bone ornament
24 Bone tube
25 Bow-shaped object of bronze

26 Domed disk of mother-of-pearl
27 Bone ornament
28 Bone tube
29 Tang of bronze arrowhead
30–31 Bronze axle-caps
32 Bone ornament
33 Eight domed disks of bronze
34 Seven domed disks of bronze
35 Bronze ring with spur
36 Bronze arrowhead
37 Bone tube
38 Bronze domed disks (about 58)
39–40 Bronze ornaments from the yoke
41–42 Harness yokes
43–44 Triangular plaques of bronze
45 Bronze domed disks (17 in number)
46 Bronze domed disks (about 58)
47–48 Bronze cheek-pieces
49–50 Bronze domed disks
51–52 Bronze ornaments from horses' foreheads

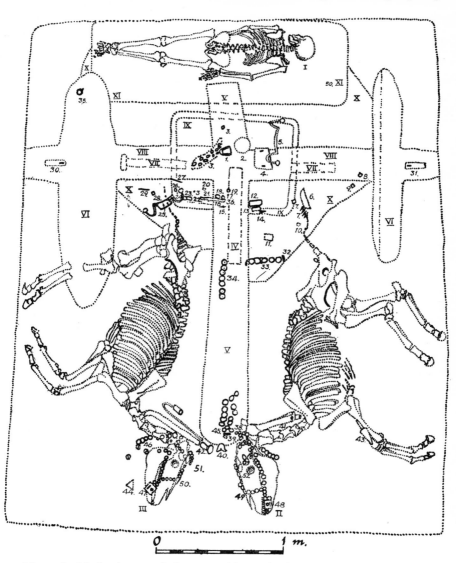

Fig. 22 Burial of a chariot, with charioteer and horses, found near Anyang, Honaen Province. Late Shang Dynasty, 12th-11th century B.C. (Pl. 11)

The bend at the end of the chariot's main shaft is inexplicable, and probably accidental. Seen from the side the shaft has a shallow double curve in the middle, designed to keep the two ends—beneath the box, and between the horses' heads—in a horizontal position. The various timbers, the crossbar of the yoke, main shaft, axle and foundation of the driver's box, can only have been lashed or pegged together with wood, for there was no trace of metal at these points. There is no indication of the shape of the box or the dashboard beyond the trace of its oblong foundation. The wheels measured 1·5 metres in diameter, their rims were about 7 cm. wide, and held without metal. Eighteen tapering spokes joined the rims to a hub about 22 cm. in diameter and some 35 cm. long. The length of the hub is understandable when it is considered that the bearing was of wood on wood, and can have been lubricated only with animal grease or pitch. The elongated hub caps, perforated to receive linch pins, are similar in design to those used afterwards, throughout the Chou dynasty.

In the Ta Ssŭ K'ung chariotgrave only one man has been sent to the Yellow Springs with the chariot he drove or commanded. He is seen lying prone behind the box. In one of the chariotpits at Hsiao T'un there were two human occupants and four horses. The normal complement, to judge from the practice of the Near East and the Greeks, would be a driver and a bowman. Like the Greeks, the Shang charioteer probably used his vehicle to approach and surprise the enemy, and dismounted for the main fight. The second pair of horses must have been harnessed to traces on either side of the pair on whose necks the yoke rested, in the manner of the Homeric *paraseiroi*.

From these excavations we cannot, unfortunately, deduce a sure answer to a crucial question: whether the harness, like that of the ancient Near East, Greece and Rome, took the draught from bands passed around the horses' necks, or included some device to enable the horses to exert their effort

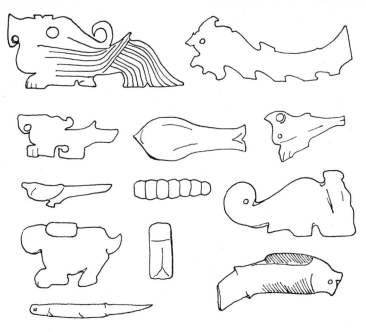

Fig. 23 Jade animal amulets. From Ta Ssŭ K'ung, Anyang. The majority are carved from thin slices of jade. Scale approx. 3:4

with the chest and shoulders. In the former case the Chinese chariot suffered from the same disability as the Western chariot: the harder the horses pulled the more they tended to choke themselves and to raise their heads into an unsuitable position for their run. From the first century B.C. the Chinese possessed a form of harness which placed the strain on the chest and shoulders and obtained a much more effective draught. This was an invention which anticipated a similar European device, the hard collar, by almost a thousand years. On the whole, it is likely that the Shang used the choker harness, otherwise four horses would hardly have been attached to a single light chariot. Of the horses themselves, pending the publication of a study of their bones, we can as yet say little. They appear to be short of stature and large-headed, and therefore probably related, as one would expect, to the steppe horse of Przewalski. The bridle did not include a bit: the material, bone or rope, which passed through the horse's mouth to join the perforated cheek-pieces which were found lying beside the jaws, had perished without trace.

The homeland of the Chou people in Shansi and Shensi provinces is more suitable for horse-raising than the Central Plain, and in historical times has supplied horses to the rest of China. It is probable, although there is no archaeological proof of this yet, that the Chou were acquainted with chariotry even before they moved east to conquer the Shang kingdom in 1027 B.C. We may imagine that the chariot played some part in their campaign. The siting of the chariot-pits at Hsiao T'un connects them with the later phase of the city, the twelfth to eleventh centuries B.C., a time when we may suppose that the Chou were already a power to be reckoned with. The resemblance of the Shang chariot to chariots made in the Near East towards the end of the second millennium B.C. is too great to be dismissed as a coincidence. If ideas of chariot design reached China from the West they probably traversed the Chou territory on their journey eastwards. It is conceivable that the Shang chariot was a borrowing from their western neighbours, on whom they may have relied besides for the supply of horses.

POTTERY

The pottery of the Shang dynasty makes on the whole a poor showing compared with the finer wares of the Neolithic period. Painting was never practised and burnishing is rare. The purely ceramic forms—the *li* and the *ting* must be included with these, though they soon came to copy the tense lines of the bronze versions—are often rough in technique and finish, and bag-shaped pots with rounded bottom are common throughout the period. The forms of *li* and *ting* descend with little change at first from the coarse grey pottery which is found in central China combined with the finer wares of both the Yang Shao and the Lung Shang Neolithic. While bronze ousted the finer neolithic pottery, the humbler tradition continued. A Shang innovation in the coarse ware was the introduction of a ring foot. The potter's wheel was used where it was appropriate, but even in rounded vessels the potter often resorted to the old method of beating out the sides with a patterned spatula, or a stick bound with cord.

Through the three stages of the Cheng Chou sites we may observe gradual changes in the proportions of pottery *ting*, *li* and *hsien*, the pedestal bowl called *tou* and the peculiar deep vase with flat base or rounded bottom which the excavators call the largemouthed *tsun*. Following the results achieved at Cheng Chou a typological study of the pottery forms has begun, but a clearer picture of the stratigraphical sequence at Hsiao T'un will be necessary before a sequence can be established for the whole of the Shang period. It is still quite uncertain whether some differences noticeable between the potteries of the two city sites are contemporary local divergencies or reflect earlier and later stages of development. The virtual absence of the *ting* from Hsiao T'un is surprising, for this type is common at Cheng Chou. The largemouthed *tsun* is also rarer at the northern city. It is strange too that the pedestal bowl should continue to be made in pottery throughout the Shang period whereas the few known bronze copies of this vessel appear all to be of early Shang date and imitate the most primitive shapes of the pottery series. The bronze *tou* in a sophisticated form and furnished with a lid makes its appearance again some 500 years later, in the late Chou period, when it figures among the ritual vessels.[10]

Fig. 24

The banality of Shang pottery is relieved by two remarkable discoveries made by Shang potters: the utilisation of pure white clay and the invention of a hard felspathic glaze. The former is

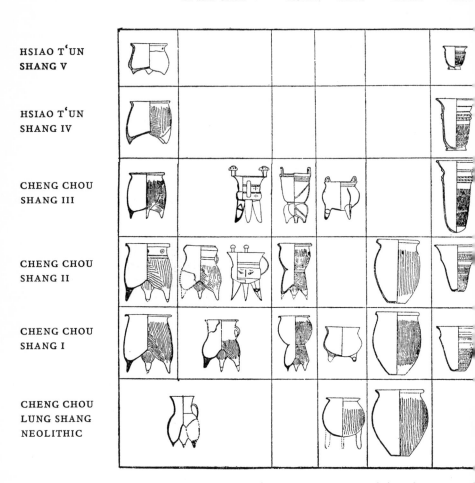

Fig. 24 *Pottery, bronzes, stone axes and oracle bones from Cheng C*

kaolin, the 'China clay' to which Chinese ceramic art owed
its supremacy two thousand years later, from the Sung period
onwards. Fragments of white ware have been found sporadic‑
ally on neolithic sites from Shangtung to Kansu, but only in

TOU	LEI	P'OU	KUEI	YÜ	STONE TOOLS BRONZE WEAPONS ORACLE BONES

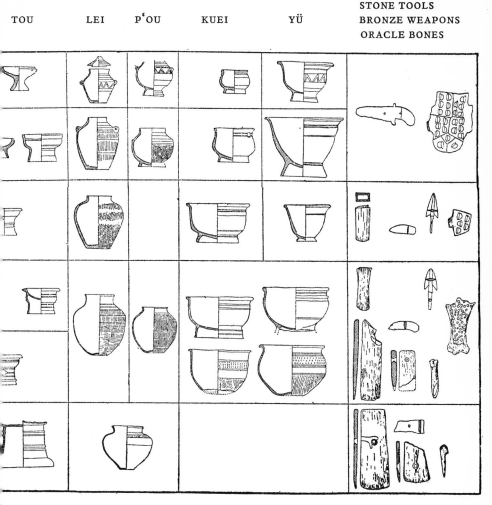

Anyang, showing the development at these sites. Not to scale. After K'ao Ku Hsüeh Pao (1956)

the Shang period (and perhaps only at Hsiao T'un) was this material deliberately exploited. It was sometimes fired to a hardness needing a kiln capable of a temperature of more than 1000 degrees centigrade. The white pots are a superior

a

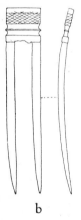

b

Fig. 25 a, b, c,
Bone pins of the
Shang period: a,
Ostasiatiska Mu-
seet, Stockholm: b,
from Hsiao T'un:

ware, decorated by carving—a technique not found on other pottery—with ornament in part identical with motifs used on the bronzes. They do not copy the bronze ornament slavishly, however, and introduce some pattern peculiar to themselves.

The glazed ware, high-shouldered bowls and vases, is equally distinctive. It has been found at Cheng Chou and Hui Hsien as well as at Hsiao T'un. The body, which also occurs unglazed, is mostly as hard as that of the white ware, but thinner, buff or grey in colour, and sometimes contains ground quartz. It is wheel-turned, impressed with small spirals or S-shaped or checker-board figures. On many pieces the glaze appears in patches, an effect which might be achieved by merely scattering wood ash on the pots as they were burnt in the kiln. But other specimens have the thin greenish-yellow glaze evenly spread on the inner and outer surfaces, and here the glaze must have been more carefully applied.

A strange light is cast on the nature of early technology by the fact that neither of these outstanding discoveries was exploited to the extent one might expect. The white ware ends with the Shang, while the glazing of pottery ceases after about 800 B.C., to reappear in different forms in the Han period. As a sub-stitute for the white marble or ivory vessels which were buried with important persons the production of the white pottery may have ceased as the fashion passed, but the advantages of a strong, thin-walled vessel made water-tight with glaze might have been expected to keep this technique alive.

Potters and bronze-smiths, like carvers of jade and bone, were organised in the Shang cities in regular workships. Such specialisation is natural to Bronze Age societies everywhere. In China, as in the Near East, the city rulers who dominated a vast peasantry slowly emerging from neolithic primitiveness enjoyed the monopoly of bronze-casting and therefore of the most effective weapons. Policy, as well as expense and the secretiveness of a difficult craft, withheld bronze from the farmers. The art of writing appears to have been in China, more than in the Mesopotamian states, a closely guarded monopoly of the ruling caste. The oracular inscriptions which survive, illuminating as they are regarding superstition, some military affairs and the acts of kings, inform us hardly at all on common life, trade, systems of land-tenure, civil rights or local government.

The method of augury so abundantly illustrated by the oracle-bones recovered at Hsiao T'un is one that survived among some primitive peoples of the Far East until recent times. The answers to questions put to the test were given by interpreting cracks produced on animal bone, usually shoulder blades, by applying a hot bronze point. No evidence of this scapulimancy has been produced from sites of the Yang Shao period, but it was practised in more primitive form at Ch'eng Tzǔ Yai and other Lung Shan settlements. On the Ch'eng Tzǔ Yai bones marks were scratched which remain undecipherable and do not seem to constitute writing. A written record of the oracle was added in later Shang times.

AUGURY

Plate 24

The choice of bone used in the process shows a gradual change from the Late Neolithic to the end of the Shang period. Goat, ox and deer shoulder-blades were used at Ch'eng Tzǔ Yai, and at the Shang I and II sites at Cheng Chou. But in the upper level of Erh Li Kang, Shang III, ox bones account for half the total recovered, and a few tortoise carapaces appear. At the People's Park site, Shang IV, it is the tortoise-shells, nearly always the lower half, which amount to half the total, and deer is virtually absent. The greater proportion of ox bones in the central Honan sites as compared with the Lung Shan sites farther east may reflect the increasing importance of cattle in the economy, but the predilection for tortoise in the Shang cities can only be ascribed to a refinement of the augur's technique. The tortoises suggest too that trade relations were

c

Fig. 25 c, Royal Ontario Museum. Scale 1:3

now established with peoples living south of the Yangtze River and in the Huai River valley, for these animals cannot have been found in the natural state farther north.

At Hsiao T'un the choice of tortoise-shell or animal bone varies at different times. Under the twenty-fourth, twenty-fifth, thirtieth and thirty-first kings tortoise predominates, but seems to have been temporarily abandoned under the twenty-eighth and twenty-ninth kings when ox bones were used almost exclusively. No specialisation according to the content of the oracular questions is noticeable, but the different materials were sometimes stored apart, as in Pits 127 and 344 in sector C, which held respectively shells and bones. Some rare inscriptions appearing only on tortoise-shells appear to record the importation of them to Hsiao T'un, although the tortoise-shell is not named in them. According to one such inscription someone had 'brought in 250 pieces'. Another places the figure 1000 after a character which is interpreted as a place-name. Allusions in literature of the late Chou period suggest that tortoise-shell augury was practised throughout the Chou Dynasty, but no evidence of it has been excavated at Chou sites. Han historians say that it was used in their time throughout the country, and that only 'eastern tribes' used bone.

The cracks on the bone or shell which the Shang augur interpreted were not allowed quite to take their own course. By boring a shallow pit, at first round and later, from Shang IV, a round pit overlapped by an oval one, the run of the lines was to some extent determined. A hot bronze point was applied on the edge of the pits and the cracks appeared on the other side. Ideally these cracks consisted of a main line with a small spur leaving it at right angles, producing the shape which was used for the character ⼘, *pu*, to divine. By a convention which now eludes us the relationship of the small cracks to the larger ones determined the answers, which might then be inscribed as 'favourable' or 'unfavourable' after the questions. A bronze drill of square section from Erh Li Kang (found with a bone on which it had been used) and a jade model of a bronze graver with sloping point of V-section from Wu Kuan Ts'un near Hsiao T'un are the only specimens of the augur's tools, but he must have used saws, knives and scrapers besides, for the carapaces were trimmed and burnished before use.

The oracle inscriptions, engraved, or, more rarely, painted on the bone or shell, are the earliest known form of Chinese writing. The principles of the script do not differ from those of the modern writing and are the same as those underlying the hieroglyphic and cuneiform writing of the Near East. Many words are written by a partial or simplified drawing of the objects or actions they denote, or represented by the picture of an object which is close to them in pronunciation. Some are abstract conventional signs. Another method was to place together two elements, one of which—e.g. 'tree', 'hand', 'water' —hinted at the associations of the word, while the other suggested the sound in the manner of a rhebus. This last procedure is rare in the oracle sentences, but later it became the most useful means of expanding the written vocabulary. In all respects the language of the oracle sentences is the Chinese of historical times, monosyllabic, uninflected and dependent on word order for relating the parts of speech. Although the principles of writing have remained basically unaltered from the Shang

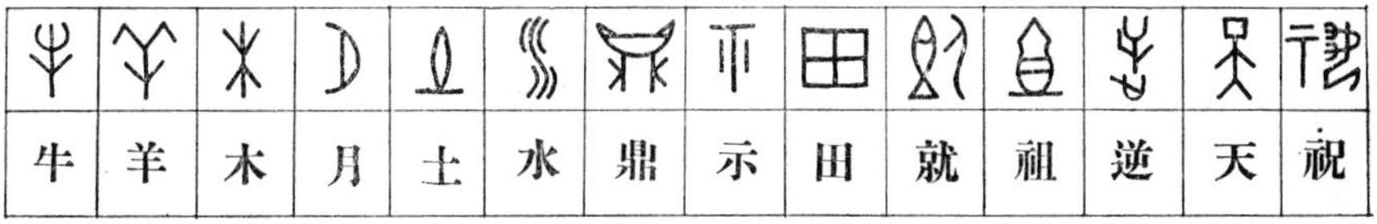

Fig. 26

Fig. 26 The earliest form of Chinese writing, as found on oracle bones, with (below) modern equivalents. Translation, from left to right: Ox; goat, sheep; tree; moon; earth; water; tripod, vessel (*ting*); to show, declare; field (showing divisions); then (man and bowl); ancestor (*phallus*); to go against, towards; heaven; to pray.

dynasty to the present day, a reform undertaken in the second century B.C. has obscured the meaning of the greater part of the oldest stock of ideographs. The interpretation of the oracle sentences turns therefore in the first place on the comparison and identification of the old forms with the later. Out of some 5000 ideographs recorded from the Shang period only about 1500 can now be convincingly interpreted, and divergent views are entertained on many characters crucial to the trans-lation of the terse oracle sentences. Even the discussion of the sentences is difficult in any language but Chinese, for the exact Shang phonetic values of the ideographs are not known, and modern Chinese words in romanised form can only be sub-stituted for the ideographs when both the meaning and the equivalence with the standard Chinese script are reasonably sure.

The main subjects on which the oracle was interrogated were the appropriateness of sacrifice to the royal ancestors, the sickness and comings and goings of the king, the advisability of undertaking hunting expeditions or of taking military action against hostile neighbours, the likelihood of rain, the success of crops and the possibility of untoward events. Questions on the last subject were generally confined to the following *hsün*, a ten-day division of the calendar. It is clear from the form of some of the longer inscriptions that the sentence engraved on the bone was a record made after the completion of the oracle-taking, for the verification of the oracle's answer is occasionally added. The brief sentences presumably note only the essence of what was spoken when the bone was burned and the cracks interpreted. Most of the sentences begin with a combination of two characters indicating a day of a 60-day cycle which was obtained by placing together and repeating in parallel a series of ten, and a distinct series of twelve, symbols.[11]

The briefest sentences consist of only two or three words: 'Rain or not?', 'Is it permissible to go forth?' But even the matter of rain might be elaborated and the verification noted, as in the following series of sentences. These are inscribed on different parts of the same ox scapula and, being dated to the same day, clearly refer to the same prognostication:

'Day *keng tzŭ*, oracle taken, *Cheng* (augur's name) asking, tomorrow, *hsin ch'ou*, will the weather be fine? asking, tomorrow, *hsin ch'ou*, will the weather not be fine?

'The king examined and said, this evening it will rain, tomorrow, *hsin ch'ou*, it will be fine.

'In that night rain was granted, on *hsin ch'ou* it was fine.'

But normally the record is briefer:

'*Kuei mao*, asking, in the (next) *hsün*, nothing untoward?'

'To Ancestor Chia (eighteenth king) a goat? To Ancestor Keng (P'an Keng, nineteenth king, founder of the city of Great Shang) a goat?'

'*Yi wei*, asking, an ox to the Thirteen Ancestors? A goat to the Lesser Ancestors?'

'Kuei mao, an oracle, asking, any harm to the king in the (next) *hsün*?'

'*Ting hai*, an oracle, asking, shall we hunt *pi lu* (Place or animal?)?'

Questions on sacrifice, of which scores of different kinds are given special names, are the most frequent of all. When the recipients were the royal ancestors their names are found to correspond closely to the king-list and the list of the pre-royal Shang ancestors preserved in the histories. The validity of the traditional list was thus dramatically vindicated, to the discomfiture of sceptical historians.[12]

The sacrifice lists distinguish between generations of kings and individuals (cf. the 'Thirteen Ancestors', i.e. the chief representatives of generations, and the 'Lesser Ancestors' in the sentence quoted). In the first half of the Hsiao T'un period the royal succession went from older to younger brother, but from father to son after the twenty-seventh king. The sacrificed animals were chiefly the ox, goat and pig—the *suovetaurilia* of

THE SHANG
STATE AS
REFLECTED
IN THE
ORACLE
SENTENCES

the Romans—though deer and dogs, and very rarely human beings, were also offered. In many of the sentences in set form there occurs between *pu* 'oracle taken' and *chen* 'asking or inter‑ preting' a character which is believed to be the name of the officiating augur. These names form distinct groups numbering from a half‑dozen to a score at different times. Tung Tso‑pin made a brilliant contribution to the study of the oracle‑bones when he made the augurs' names the basis of a chronological division. He divided the reign of the Shang kings at Hsiao T'un into five periods:

   I twenty‑second king
  II twenty‑third and twenty‑fourth kings
 III twenty‑fifth to twenty‑sixth kings
 IV twenty‑seventh to twenty‑eighth kings
  V twenty‑ninth to thirtieth kings

and so much enhanced the historical value of the information which is gleaned from the oracle records.

The first of these periods, that of the King Wu Ting (sixteenth or early fifteenth century B.C.), has produced the greatest number of sentences concerned with military enter‑ prises. The common form of question asks for the auspices regarding the chastisement of an entity which appears as two characters, the first a proper name and the second the word *fang*, meaning direction or region. Of the proper names more than a dozen occur with some frequency and clearly refer to tribes with whom the Shang were at enmity. The study of these names in connexion with later literary traditions sug‑ gests that the majority of them inhabited the region lying to the north‑west of the Shang capital, in what is now south and east Shansi. Written history confirms that Shang power had begun to expand in this direction in the earlier part of the dynastic reign. The locations given of capitals that were occupied before P'an Keng's move to Hsiao T'un are in some instances obscure, but several seem to have been in eastern

Honan and one (Yen, cited in the Bamboo Annals) was in Shantung.[13] The move to Hsiao T'un thus seems to have been an advance to the west and north-west.

It is difficult to say quite what is meant by the alleged peregrination of the Shang rulers, whether the moves involved considerable numbers of people or, as seems more likely, only the settlement of the ruling house at different points in a large territory which they dominated. Perhaps the flooding of the Yellow river, or a superstition connected with the king's death, were contributing reasons. Students of the oracle sentences infer that the influence of the Shang kings made itself felt through most of central China, including the provinces of Shantung, Honan and Hopei, and even extended into the northern part of Anhui and Kiangsu. Sites of Shang date, identified by pottery and minor relics, are being excavated at the present time over the whole of this area, and as methods of dating within the Shang period are refined, it may prove possible to trace the spread of Shang power archaeologically from its centre in Shantung and Honan to the outlying regions.

Apart from the historical records of the moves of the kings, the chronological succession recently established between the cities at Cheng Chou and Hsiao T'un hints at a move of the centre of power northwards in Honan in the middle of the Shang period. The expansion towards the north-west seems to have encountered the opposition of the Shansi tribes and to have stopped on the line of the T'ai Hang mountains. Beyond this mountain barrier and farther west along the Yellow river and its tributaries dwelt tribes who appear in history as the Chou confederacy, and whose eastward advance overthrew the Shang and occupied their capital in 1027 B.C. Already in the time of Wu Ting there is mention of a Chou chieftain allied to the Shang. At this time the Shang king is preoccupied with attacks in the north-west of his territory. In oracle-bone periods IV and V, the age of the last four kings, in the late twelfth and eleventh centuries B.C., the military oracles are chiefly con/ cerned with hostile peoples who appear to inhabit the east or south/east. It appears from an inscription on a bronze vessel found in Shantung that Chao, the last of his line, undertook a major expedition to the east. It may have been this distraction which gave the Chou their opportunity.[14]

In the light of the oracle sentences, perhaps inevitably from the nature of them, the Shang state appears as a kind of theo/ cracy. The king might himself act as an augur, increasingly so in the later periods of the oracle sentences. He is assisted, be/ sides the named augurs, by other individuals designated by names of which some are applied also to the shamans and ritualists recorded in the earliest Chinese literature. The activity of priests of this kind may have included the ecstatic trance and communication with the world of spirits and ghosts which is still the rôle of the village medicine/man in some primitive communities of the Far East. In the official religion the royal ancestors are gods whose favour must be ensured, but their powers appear to be less than those of the deity called Shang Ti, i.e. Supreme Ruler, who is able to visit the state with storm and blight of crops and other disasters. Some of the sacrifices reflect animistic beliefs which, like the presence of shamans, suggest the nature of the popular religion over which the official system was raised. Heavenly beings who received sacrifice were, besides Shang Ti, the Sun, Clouds, Rain, Wind and Snow, and the Western Mother and Eastern Mother. Gods of the earth were Earth itself (denoted by a symbol later used in the meaning of altar, originally representing perhaps an earth mound), the Four Directions, the Mountains and Rivers.

In outlying territories the Shang kings appear to have exer/ cised their power through officers who figure in the oracle sentences under the titles of Ho, Po and T'ien. At the end of the Shang period at least, they stood to the king and each other in some kind of feudal subordination, and so foreshadowed the more developed feudalism of the Chou. On the border of the Shang country were the 'regions', *fang*, some of which accepted Shang suzerainty, while others periodically were at war with the central power. The wisdom of calling on the local territorial rulers to join in a royal punitive expedition was also put to the oracular test:

'Ting Mao. The King took an oracle and interpreted. Shall we join our force of T'ien to our force of the Po and punish the Po of the Yü region?'[15]

There is evidence of slavery, with which some officials named in the sentences seem to be specially concerned. The various terms which are interpreted as denoting classes of slaves may reflect distinctions of status among them. The holocausts observed at royal funerals show how human beings, whether they were slaves or prisoners of war, might be sacrificed as chattels. But it is difficult to accept the view now adopted by Chinese authorities of a 'slave-state', with the implication that systematic slavery was the basis of the economy. On the other hand the oracle sentences tell us nothing of peasants beyond the mention of the grains which they cultivated. There is slight evidence in the sentences that irrigation was practised, though the great concern with the prognostication of rain and the prospering of crops suggest that it was not very extensive. The identification of characters denoting grain is beset with doubts. Varieties of millet are believed to have provided the main crops and the mention of rice, which could hardly be cultivated without carefully controlled irrigation, is uncertain. As in the picture we have formed of Bronze Age communities in the West, the life of the peasants of Shang times is little more known to us than that of their neolithic forebears. They continued to cultivate with stone hoes and digging sticks, and to reap with stone knives. Before the spread of iron, metal was not available to them. The kings of Shang, with their extravagant hunting expeditions, their bloody funeral pomp, their charioteers, their priest-like rôle and eventual deification, are the more familiar figures of the Bronze Age world, both east and west.

The bronze vessels consigned to Shang graves were primarily instruments of sacrifice, but they fulfilled also a social rôle, survived the fall of Shang and attained political importance in Chou times. The Shang vessels sometimes have a brief inscription appropriating them for sacrifice to a particular an-cestor, the individual being denoted by one of the calendar series of ten symbols. The briefest inscriptions name the maker by a single character, stating that he 'made a precious sacrificial vessel for (sacrifice to) Ancestor (e.g.) Ting'. Often this for-mula is preceded or followed by an emblem, distinct from the ideographs of the ordinary script. Sometimes only the emblem appears, or the maker's name, or 'vessel' with the ancestor's ritual calendar symbol. Although the theory is now rejected that the emblematic characters are totemic marks, it seems clear that they are a personal designation of some kind, probably the signature of a clan or great family. On a few vessels assigned to the latest decades of Shang a fuller formula appears, e.g.:

'*Keng shen*. The King was in the East Hall. The King augustly came. The Minister Hu followed him. He be-stowed 5 strings of cowrie shells. They were used to make a sacrificial vessel for Ancestor *Ting*. In the 6th month, in the King's 25th year . . .'

The inscription describes a royal award of cowries, a form of currency (or at least a valuation of goods), and the recipient, using the gift to honour an ancestor, has recorded it and announced it piously to his ancestors. The dedicatory texts, far more frequent, in which there is no question of a royal gift, suggest that some form of clan organisation persisted in the upper class of the Shang population and was the basis of an ancestor worship like that practised by the kings.

Chapter III

The Later Bronze Age: the Chou Dynasty

THE CONQUEST OF THE Shang territory by the rulers of the house of Chou and the political arrangements which ensued have been regarded by Confucian historians as a revolutionary upheaval, the most important event in the early history of China. According to historical tradition the motive for the Chou attack was to chastise the Shang king for his debauchery and neglect of the public weal. Moral justification of this kind is propagated in the older parts of the Shu Ching, which were composed in the early decades of Chou rule. It is found also in inscriptions cast on bronze vessels in the reigns of the earliest Chou kings. The Chou were later believed to be the originators of the feudal order which they instituted and therefore the fountain-head of the public and private loyalties upon which Confucius founded his ethical system. Yet because a reigning dynasty must be recognised as culturally superior to the peoples of the outer territories of the empire, the Chou are presented at once as political saviours and, until the eve of their conquest, as cultural barbarians. There are indications that this was not so, but the archaeological evidence for the cultural status of the western region during the Shang period is still very slight. It is perhaps in this direction that the most interesting discoveries concerning the origins of Bronze Age culture in China will be made in the future.

THE FEUDAL EMPIRE OF THE CHOU

From the histories and from the Shang oracle sentences something can be gleaned of the earlier history of the Shangs' dynastic successors. The centre of the Chou kingdom lay at first in western Shensi, on the upper courses of the Ching and Wei rivers, in upland country suitable for both agriculture and droving. The Chou potentate mentioned in oracle sentences of the time of the Shang king Wu Ting is called 'hou' ('marquis') and seems to belong to a group of local rulers so designated who normally accepted the suzerainty of Shang. In the case of Chou it must have been an uneasy submission from the start. One sentence queries the auspices of a punitive expedi‚ tion by the Shang king against the Chou, in which the forces of the royal clan were to be joined to those of a *hou* called Ch'üan. The latter, in the light of later tradition, may denote the ruler of nomadic peoples in the north‚west, probably occupying the northern tracts of Shansi and Shensi.[1]

The Chou were apparently experiencing pressure from this quarter themselves. They were at first obliged to move west‚ wards and later to the south, farther downstream on the Shensi rivers. Here, in the vicinity of the modern Si‚an Fu, were built the cities of Feng and Hao. From these the campaign against the Shang kingdom was eventually launched. The Chou state was powerful enough even by the middle of the Shang period to arouse the fears of the kings of the Central Plain and provoke an attack by them. An enemy who could threaten the Shang state must have possessed bronze weapons, and a considerable military organisation. Even after the conquest of 1027 B.C. the Chou kings remained in their capital in south Shensi. The fortress city of Ch'eng Chou (not to be confused with Cheng Chou!) which they built in Honan near Loyang, from which to dominate the Central Plain, remained a secondary capital until 771 B.C. Then the loss of the western territories to invading Jung nomads, a reversal aided by a palace intrigue, confined the kings to the Honan capital and made of it the centre of the Chou state. This event is taken to mark the divi‚ sion between a Western Chou and an Eastern Chou period (1027–771, 771–222 B.C.).

The forces led by the Chou king Wu Wang against Shang consisted of a federation of tribes, some of whom appear to have been of Turkish or Tibetan origin. But the bulk of people over whom the Chou kings ruled in their western homeland cannot have been nomadic. In the Shang texts the Chou are denoted by an ideograph (which is the character still used) representing a square field divided into four. It is quite likely that the choice of the symbol was an allusion to their practice of agriculture, a recognition that the Chou, like the Shang themselves and unlike the majority of the Shang's enemies, based their power on a farming peasantry. In contrast to this, the term *ch'üan*, 'dog', used to denote the people whom Wu Ting was prepared to use in an attack on Chou, may allude to their nomadic life, in which the dog was specially important for droving.

Upon the defeat of the Shang king his son was enfeoffed by Wu Wang in part of the central Shang territory in Honan. Shortly afterwards Wu Wang's son and successor Ch'eng Wang, assisted by Wu Wang's brother, the Duke of Chou, who acted as regent, was obliged to crush a Shang revolt. The Shang vassal was executed and a Chou ruler, another royal brother, was set over his territory as marquis of the feudal state of Wei. Other members and relatives of the Chou royal clan were set over the states of Yen (Hopei), Lu (Shantung), and Ch'i (Shansi). These four were the first great feudatories. Under them were eventually ranged hundreds of small city fiefs. The first concern of the Chou leaders, as of the leaders of the nomads' armies in Asia in later times, was to reward the commanders who had served under them. The whole of northern China was garrisoned by troops loyal to the Chou king, whose own territory under direct rule was confined to the region around the eastern capital at Loyang.

The Chou partitioning of the empire into fiefs and the institution of five classes of hereditary nobility continued a method of decentralising power which we see foreshadowed in Shang times. It was now more minutely and systematically regulated. Obeisance and tribute passed up the ranks of the feudal hierarchy to the king at the top. The nobles were required to

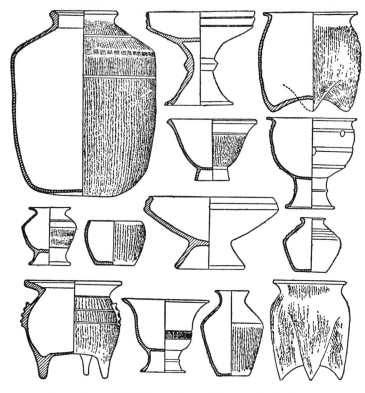

Fig. 27 Pottery of the Western Chou period, late 11th-early 8th centuries B.C. Scale approx. 1:10

journey periodically to the capital. But in practical affairs the attention of the feudatories was more taken up with the subjection and administration of the lands granted them in fief.

Although the feudal states were under an obligation to supply garrison troops to the Chou king, no large army was permitted to be formed under his control. Military assistance was lent to the king by the states acting independently. In this lay the germ of the inter-state rivalries, the leaguing together, the creation of new states and the swallowing up of older ones which determined the course of Chinese history for eight hundred years. From the start the king in his north-eastern home was at a disadvantage, for he was nearest at hand to stem the inroads of nomads, badly placed to enforce his policies on the feudatories, and, having a greater proportion of semi-nomadic people in his territory, perhaps less able to build his power upon a settled peasantry than were the feudal rulers of the eastern parts of the Central Plain. Even the semblance of a central power passes with the defeat of King Yu in 771 B.C. and the move of his successor P'ing to the capital at Loyang. The territory he relinquished, reconquered from the pretender and his barbarian supporters, became the fief of Ch'in, whose expansion westwards centuries later was to close the chapter of feudal history and unite the empire under a single command.

Fig. 28

In the centuries after 771 B.C. some score of feudal states contended together, using the apparatus of feudal allegiance to Chou as a means to their own ends. The Chou king for a while could ally himself with the strongest contender. The hegemony fell at first to the eastern state of Ch'i, which had enlarged its territory by conquering the whole of the Shantung peninsula and by its position astride water routes had become an important centre of trade. It also benefited from a state-organised monopoly of salt, produced from the sea—an advantage which Chou itself is said to have enjoyed in the Fen River valley of its homeland. From Ch'i the hegemony passed to other northern states, all of which were gradually compelled to sink their differences as a threat grew from Ch'u. This was a state established in the lower Yangtze basin, forming the southern limit of the empire, which was regarded as semi-barbarous. In the fifth century it began to expand its power to the north, overthrew the states of Wu and Yüeh and proceeded to engulf the smaller states of the Central Plain south of the Yellow river. This encroachment was destined to be arrested only by the even more explosive expansion of Ch'in from its western highlands in the earlier part of the third century B.C.

Meanwhile provocation from 'barbarians' in the north-west, particularly from the nomads of southern Shansi, inter-mittently put the Chou king and his neighbouring feudatories in peril. In 660 B.C. the invaders succeeded in occupying the capital of the state of Wei in Honan, putting to flight its gar-rison. By this time the Chou king was stripped of real power, though a ceremonial allegiance to him was professed. In 704 B.C. the ruler of Ch'u had arrogated the title of Wang, king, an action which spelled the decline even of the formal feudal ties. Nevertheless the integrity of the Chou state was respected until 256 B.C., when it fell a prey to Ch'in.

RELIGION
AND FEUDAL
CEREMONIAL
The Chou feudatories, as free princes, exercised auto-cratic rule from their walled cities. Unfortunately the histories tell us nothing of land tenure or legal systems which might throw light on their closer relations with their subjects. Taxa-tion and conscription could be aggravated to the point of raising rebellion. We learn nothing of traditional communal rights allowed to the peasantry. In theory it seems that government in each state was absolute and centralised. Slavery, domestic and agricultural, continued. There is no evidence that it was regulated in the legal system. The population below the aristo-cracy was divided by the theorists into educated gentry (*shih*), peasant farmers (*nung*), artisans and merchants (*shang*). The subordination of the merchant class to the rest was more than theoretical. The control of trade, state monopoly in salt and later in iron, was an important feature of the economy of the city state. The prerogative of the feudal rulers descended theo-retically from the king, who in turn had received the mandate of Heaven. The only threat the reformer might voice was that this mandate could be withdrawn, that unrest among the people was a sign that this was imminent. The concept of Heaven as a ruling supernatural power, and the designation of

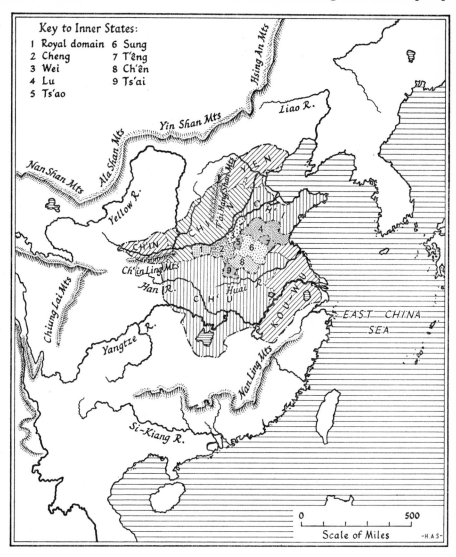

Fig. 28 China's physical features and the feudal states

the king as the Son of Heaven, seem to be ideas introduced by the Chou. They are perhaps a legacy of the religion of the nomads of inner Asia.

The official religion had freed itself from obligation to the many deities celebrated by the Shang, and required sacrifice principally to Heaven (which was evidently equated with the Shang Ti of the Shang) and to Earth. Divination of the kind attested by the oracle-bones in the Shang period can no longer be traced in excavated material, and, judging from inscriptions preserved on bronze vessels, seems no longer to have been a direct concern of the kings. The cult of royal ancestors also ceases as an important part of the state religion, but the tradition of family piety finds its expression in the ancestor cult which had already taken root at the beginning of the Chou era. Although this cult would seem natural to a society of the patriarchal, nomadic kind which is claimed for the Chou people in their homeland, we need not suppose that the Chou were responsible for introducing it into central China. The germ of ancestor worship existed in Shang times.

In the elaborate ceremonial which was observed at the courts of the Chou king and the feudal princes, the award of honours recorded in inscriptions cast on bronze vessels holds the greatest interest for the archaeologist. The custom seems to have begun before the fall of the Shang dynasty (see p. 108) and it can be traced through the whole of the Western Chou period. Under the Chou kings, particularly in the first few reigns, the inscriptions are often long and circumstantial, and contain important historical information. The ceremonial of award had become the symbol of the political bond between Chou and the feudal states, The award might be from the king, or from a feudatory to a subordinate, and the recipient is appointed to a fief, or an office, perhaps given a new noble title; his devotion in service may be commented on and a moral exhortation bestowed along with the material gifts. More rarely the inscription is cast to commemorate an important event or campaign without awards to individuals; more rarely still, to set down the regu/ lation of a boundary. The bronze made to mark the occasion of the gift is usually designated in the inscription as a 'precious vessel' destined for use in sacrifice to ancestors, to a named indi/ vidual. Often inscriptions contain no more than this dedication.

In the reigns of kings Ch'eng and K'ang (late eleventh and early tenth centuries B.C.) the king is found speaking and making the award in person. Thereafter the phraseology of the inscriptions shows that the king, even if present, allowed the pronouncement of the award to be made by one of his officers. The text, written on the bamboo slips of which the books of the time were made, was handed by the king to an officer who read it aloud. In one instance the king appears with an officer on either side of him, one of whom handed him the bamboo brevet, which he then handed to a second officer to be read out.[2] The king is generally stated to be in his capital and in a great hall of his palace. There, with his assistants, he faced south, while the recipient of the award was introduced by a special officer and stood facing the king. After the citation the recipient carried away the bamboo brevet and presumably the material gifts also.

One of the longest and most circumstantial texts is that in/ scribed on the 'Great Yü Ting', cast in the time of the third Chou king, K'ang, who reigned for some thirty years at the beginning of the tenth century B.C. It was found in 1821 near Mei Hsien in Shensi. The brevet falls into four sections, begin/ ning with the moralising eulogy of the Chou victory which is customary in the early decades of the Chou. Then follow the bestowal—or confirmation—of the fief, an appointment to office, and a list of gifts:

'In the 9th month, the King being in Tsung Chou [i.e. the western capital near Loyang] conferred a brevet on Yü. The king had spoken thus: "Yü, the glorious king Wen [i.e. the last of the predynastic rulers of Chou] received the great order of Heaven. When King Wu succeeded him he established our empire. He abolished their [the Shangs'] iniquities and extended our rule to the four quarters. He imposed order on their subjects. In exercising the kingly office he did not presume to abuse the use of wine, nor to disturb the customary sacrifices. Therefore Heaven protected its son. Heaven also defended the former king [i.e. the second king, Ch'eng] . . . to rule the four quarters. We have learned that the kings of Shang had forfeited the mandate of Heaven. The great feudatories and the royal officers of Shang were reckless in their use of wine, and so the empire was lost to them.

'"You, Yü, from your youth have shown great devotion in service. You [have been our mentor?] and devoted your energies to us. We model our government on the virtuous principles of King Wen. . . . And now we enjoin on you to be the assistant of Yung, cleaving to virtue and wisdom. Be diligent day and night to advise your sovereign fearlessly. . . . The king said, I command Yü to assume the heritage of his ancestor the duke of Nan. During the rest of your lifetime you shall be the lieutenant of Hsia in the control of affairs affecting the Jung barbarians. Diligently punish offenders, day and night assist your sovereign in the command of the empire. Thus I shall preserve the rule and the territory bequeathed to me by my royal ancestors.

'"We bestow on you a wine goblet for sacrifice, a headdress and robe; also the duke of Nan's chariot banner for use in hunting. I bestow on you likewise four Pang Ssŭ, with men, from charioteers to common people, six hundred and fifty-nine; likewise thirteen Shih Ssŭ, with one thousand and fifty men . . . from their land.

'"Yü, maintain your probity, do not disregard this our command."

'Yü returned thanks to the king, and, receiving the honour, had a precious *ting* made for [sacrifice to] the duke of Nan. In the twenty-third year of the king's reign.'

The bestowal of men seen here is usually taken to indicate slavery, but it is possible that some form of feudal subordination is involved. Pang Ssŭ and Shih Ssŭ are titles of officers, the former possibly territorial and the latter military, and since each is followed by a number of men it would appear that they are in command over these. Unfortunately the two characters preceding the phrase 'from their land' have not so far yielded any sure sense. Could they be interpreted, some light might be thrown on the feudal status of these subordinates. In the inscription on the *kuei* of the Marquis of Hsing, preserved in the British Museum, the gift of slaves is, however, explicit: 'I bestow on you the three classes of slaves . . .'[3]

Plates 34, 35

As an example of an inscription affording important historical information none better can be cited than that on a bronze kuei excavated in 1954 at Yen Tun Shan in Kiangsu.[4] It records a sacrifice made by Ch'eng, the second Chou king, to his father Wu, speaks of the 'subjugation of the Shang' by Ch'eng—here the suppression of the Shang rebellion—and states that Ch'eng visited the eastern region. A fief is granted to Nieh in Yi, in which the find-place of this bronze and its fellows presumably lay. This corroborates the historical record of Ch'eng Wang's campaign in eastern China, and shows that already in his time political control had been extended to the east coast in the region of the Yangtze mouth. Such contemporary mention of Ch'eng's campaign suggests also that the king acted independently, and not under the regency of his uncle the duke of Chou, whose prestige and political rôle later Confucian historians were at pains to aggrandise.

Plate 33

Eventually similar ceremonies and awards came to be observed by the feudal princes, though not before the central authority had begun to decline and the feudal territories began to assume the character of independent states. Few of the bronzes cast at the feudal courts can be dated before about 950 B.C. The majority fall after the end of the Western Chou period, i.e. 771 B.C. Vessels with brief inscriptions naming feudal rulers are characteristic of the seventh to fifth centuries, when the Chou king is no longer mentioned. This political disinte/ gration is reflected also in the rise of regional artistic styles.

FORTIFIED
CITIES
    The early and middle centuries of the Chou period are so far sparsely documented by scientific excavation, although many bronze vessels belonging to this period have found their way into collections. The early Chou cities of Kao and Feng are not even precisely located. Of the eastern capital, Ch'eng Chou, some sign has, however, been found near Loyang in Honan. Sections of rammed/earth wall 3–6 metres wide are be/ lieved to belong to it. The garrison towns of the early Chou period were not sited on hills and eminences apart from modern habitation like the Iron Age forts of Europe, nor at places sub/ sequently depopulated like the tells of the Near East. They stood on rivers and other routes at places still occupied by modern towns, where excavation and even detection is diffi/ cult. We can readily imagine that in the early centuries of the Chou period, which in central China at least were compara/ tively peaceful, the function of the town as a political and economic centre outweighed its strategic importance. But these circumstances changed in the fifth and fourth centuries. The internecine warfare of the feudal states, now feudal only in name, removed the last traces of the order established by the Chou settlement. Almost every state found itself at some time embattled against its neighbours, and the smaller ones were successively engulfed by the greater. Archaeological work on accessible ancient city sites of the later Chou period has not been carried very far and we still depend largely for our informa/ tion on brief surveys made by the Japanese during their occu/ pation of the country. These surveys were confined to the pro/

vinces of Hopei and Shantung, in the territory of Yen, Ch'i and Lu, states which did not lose their independence until the second half of the third century B.C. The impressive scale of their fortifications commemorates the threat they faced before the Ch'in unification, and is perhaps the reason for their long survival.

Not all of the fortified cities adopted the rectangular plan which was used at Cheng Chou in the Shang period. The 'Lower Capital' (Hsia Tu) of the north-western state of Yen— one of the seven paramount states of the Warring States period —has an irregular perimeter formed of straight sections of wall. The area it enclosed is the largest of those which have been traced in their entirety, its greatest width measuring over 7 kilometres. The wall was build of successive layers of rammed earth, on which no traces of harder revetment have survived. At one point it still rises to a height of 10 metres on a base of 7 metres. Partly within the perimeter and partly outside, near the wall, are more than fifty rectangular earth platforms similarly constructed, which formed the foundations of important build-ings. The largest, situated beyond the wall some 800 metres to the north-west, has an area of some 1000 square metres. The part of a small river which traverses the city was confined in straight artificial banks.

In the same province of Hopei are the ruins of an earth-walled city which preserves the rectangular plan and formal layout of a more typical Chou capital. This is Chao Wang *Fig. 29* Ch'eng—the City of the Kings of Chao—at Han Tan. The state of Chao, formed in Shansi and Honan from the terri-tory of Chin at the end of the fifth century, was compelled to transfer its capital twice in the first two decades of its existence, its second eastward move bringing it to Han Tan in 386 B.C. Its surviving walls enclose two rectangular areas, adjacent on east and west. The chronological relation of the two enclosures has not been established, and it is possible that the smaller one to the east was not completed. The western enclosure is a square of sides measuring approximately 1400 metres, orient, ated to the cardinal points. The wall survives to a height of 10 metres at some places, but is estimated to have stood originally on a base some 20 metres wide and to have risen to about 15 metres. The sides are believed to have had a single slope, only slightly inclined from the vertical.

The south-facing plan of a Chou capital, as described in late-Chou texts and followed in historical times, seems to have been reversed at Chao Wang Ch'eng. The largest of the internal earth foundations lies nearer to the south wall, and whereas the north wall had three gateways—the middle one on the central axis—the south wall had only two, symmetrically sited, one third of the wall length from either end. The placing of other building foundations on the line of the north–south axis is in keeping with the ritual pattern. The largest foundation marks the position of the king's palace.

Other cities in Shantung, the capital of Ch'i at Lin Tzŭ and that of Lu at Ch'ü Fu, were protected by similar massive earth walls, those of the latter having a quite irregular shape. None of the plans appears to have been dictated by features of the terrain useful for the protection of the cities. In the flat country of the plain only the courses of minor rivers could serve this purpose. Towers and breastworks must have been built on the top of the wall, but no trace of these is visible on the surviving sections. It is interesting to find farther to the south, near Ch'ung Chou in Kiangsu province, a type of fortress uninfluenced by the traditions of the Central Plain. Here two very irregular concentric earth ramparts are combined with wide moats to protect a central citadel.

ARCHITEC, TURE The areas enclosed by the city walls we have described have been given over to tillage for two thousand years. Apart from the foundation platforms of the major buildings no external signs of streets or houses remain. We need not suppose that the

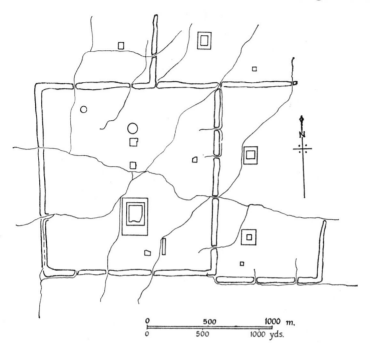

Fig. 29 Plan of remains of Chao Wang Ch'eng, capital of the Chao state. 4th century B.C.

whole or even, in the case of the larger perimeters, the greater part of the area was covered with buildings. As in the Japanese imperial capital at Nara, built at the beginning of the eighth century A.D. on the Chinese model, the major buildings may have risen above cropped fields and orchards. On the founda‚ tion platforms the only surviving building materials are frag‚ ments of curved roofing tiles and occasionally expanses of paving tiles. The date of the introduction of roofing tiles is still uncertain. There is no evidence that they were in use earlier than the fourth century B.C., when their adoption probably marked the first advance in roofing methods since the Shang period. The circular or more often semicircular ends of the eave tiles are decorated with figures of dragons or *t'ao t'ieh* monster masks in the same styles as on the contemporary bronze vessels.

On the form of wooden architecture of the Chou dynasty we should be little better informed than on the architecture of the Shang period, were it not for the architectural designs engraved on a few fragments of bronzes. The most important of these is on the sides of a bronze bowl recovered from one of the late-Chou tombs at Hui Hsien in Honan. In spite of the spatial liberties the artist has allowed himself, the relative scale of the building and the human figures may be nearly true. The excavation of one of the foundations in the Chao Wang Ch'eng revealed footing-stones of sizes which could have carried pillars no larger than those shown in the picture.

The apparent superposition of one building over another as seen here is also explained by the Chao Wang Ch'eng excavations. Here it appeared that the foundation mound was stepped on the east and west sides, the central portion standing at least 2 metres above the level of the lower foundation and separated from it by a vertical rise of rammed earth. The size of the stone footings on the lower foundation indicates slender pillars which can hardly have risen to the full height of the central structure. It appears from these features that the building on the central part of the foundation stood above two lateral galleries whose single-slope roofs rose little if at all above the height of its floor. On another scrap of bronze, found at Ch'ang Chih in Shansi, which is decorated with an all but identical picture, the roof of the lower part of the building is shown ending precisely at the floor level of the upper building. In the Chinese architecture of later times a gallery with lean-to roof surrounding the main structure is a common feature, although then it shares the same floor level. What at first appears to be the structure of these late-Chou buildings, i.e. pillars springing from

Fig. 30

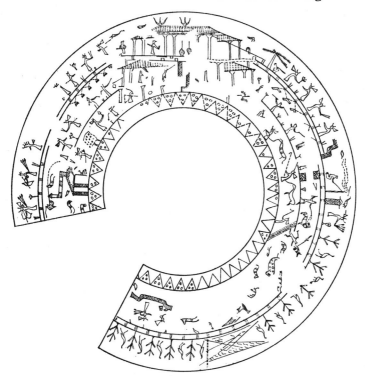

Fig. 30 Engraved decoration of a bronze bowl found at Chao Ku Hui Hsien, Honan. The activities represented included hunting, the striking of bronze bells and musical stones, and possibly rites of sacrifice. Scale 1:5

a floor which is itself carried on pillars, was never a method used in the wooden architecture of the Far East.

In both bronze pictures the main building, raised above its surrounding gallery, is surrounded also on its own level by a similar gallery whose roof slopes into the line of the main roof. At the gable ends and at the centre of the latter are horn-shaped ornaments showing an earlier form of the single-horn acroteria which appear on pottery models of buildings of the Han period and became a regular feature of the traditional architecture.

As in the Han buildings, the roof lines are straight. The up/
ward curves of the eaves which to Western eyes is the most
characteristic feature of Chinese building, was adopted later,
probably not before the Tʻang period. The tops of the pillars
are expanded in the Chou buildings by means of simple, un/
adorned capitals. If the drawings on bronze have not tended to
simplify because of their small size, we must assume that the
more elaborate, bracketed capitals of Han buildings were an
innovation of that period. In the pictures the walls are left out
to reveal the interior. Probably, as we may see a few centuries
later, wooden or plaster partitions closing the spaces between
the outer pillars were decorated with painted or openwork
designs of the kind which appears beneath the upper eaves in
the drawing.

From the pottery models of houses preserved in Han tombs
we may see some features of this architecture applied to simpler
dwellings, the homesteads and farmhouses of the peasants.
In these, as in the village architecture of China until recent
times, earth walls were the rule, only the form of the roof
showing greater sophistication. To know something of the
humbler houses of the Chou period we must await the result
of further excavation. But we may picture a majority of the
buildings in the Chou cities as single/storied huts, often set in
groups like the villages of the countryside, among fields still
cultivated within the perimeter. Here and there rose the great
palaces and halls with their ornate roofs. These looked down
broad avenues to the gates, where, under the towering walls,
peasants from the surrounding region gathered in the markets.

TOMBS OF
THE CHOU
PERIOD
    The tombs of the earlier Chou period reveal no sudden
departure from those we have described from Shang times.
Many great tombs of the early centuries must have been opened
to yield the large numbers of bronze vessels and weapons which
are preserved in modern collections, but of all these only one
description has been published. This is at Hsin Tsʻun, near

Chün Hsien in Honan, probably the burial of a prince of the ruling house of Wei, in whose territory it is situated. It follows the design of a Shang royal grave. North and south from the stepped central pit sloping passages led to the surface. The bronze vessels it contained point to a date early in the tenth century B.C. Some dozen chariots were buried and over seventy horses, together with the bronze ornaments of the vehicles and harness. The smaller graves of the eleventh and early tenth centuries as excavated at Loyang continue the shape of the Shang pit, having stepped sides. The grave-goods of pottery and bronze vessels were laid either on the shelf, or some-times at one end of the lower part of the pit, outside the wooden coffin. Beneath the coffin some graves still have the basal sacrificial pit in which the bones of a dog have been found. The size of the pits seldom exceeded 4 by 2 metres with a depth up to 3 metres, the longer axis being generally orientated approximately north and south. The body was laid supine,with the head to the north; burial in the prone position in the Shang manner is now quite exceptional. No trace survives of a mound or any other distinguishing marks on the surface.

Before the sixth to fifth centuries B.C. the only variation of the tomb pit is a changed arrangement of the stepped sides. A tomb excavated at P'u Tu Ts'un near Ch'ang An in Shensi, in the heart of the Chou homeland, shows the rise of one such minor feature which became an established custom in the north-west. The style of the bronze vessels is that of the later tenth century B.C. and the inscription on one of them points to the reign of King Mu. Only the longer, east and west, sides of the pit are stepped, and the shelves end a metre short of the south side. In one of the lateral recesses so formed were stacked the bronze vessels. In the smaller Honan and Shensi tombs of the fifth and fourth centuries B.C. the recess for the grave-goods is often excavated as a niche or even a short tunnel opening from the side of the main pit; or the niche or

Fig. 31

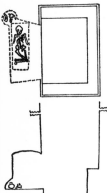

tunnel may be large enough to accommodate the main or a secondary burial.

The main occupant of the P'u Tu Ts'un grave was laid with his head to the south, and his mouth had been filled with fragments of jade-like stone. Beneath, in a basal pit of careful construction lay the dog, accompanied by two cowrie shells. On the floor of the north end of the pit, presumably outside the wooden coffin, were two human skeletons, presumably of funeral victims, laid in a crouched position. The fifteen bronze and seventeen pottery vessels comprised a full array of the sacrificial forms.

The burial of a body on its side, with crouched or flexed legs, as seen at P'u Tu Ts'un, continues a burial rite observed in some neolithic graves of north-west China. No crouched burials were found in the Shang graves of Honan, where even the slaughtered victims of the great tombs were laid extended. Nor in the tombs of the Kuo state at Shang Ts'un Ling in the same province, dating from the eighth to seventh centuries B.C. In the fifth- and fourth-century graves of Shensi it is particularly common, and by this time had spread into Honan. At Shao Kou near Loyang 104 out of 112 graves contained crouched burials.

Fig. 31 Plan and elevation of tomb with recess exca-vated at Pan P'o Ts'un, Shensi pro-vince. 4th century B.C.

Scale approx. 1:90

Other departures from the normal burial rite of the Central Plain may be seen in graves of the sixth to fifth centuries in the north-western province of Hopei, as exemplified at a ceme-tery site at T'ang Shan. Here a box formed of thin stone slabs set on edge takes the place of the wooden coffin, or the body is placed in two large pottery urns set mouth to mouth. The state of Yen, which comprised the territory of the modern Hopei province, reveals a foreign influence in the figured decoration of some of its bronze vessels. Flexed burials in slab-built chambers are characteristic of tombs of the Early Bronze culture of Karassuk in southern Siberia, whither we can trace a few other connexions of the Chinese Bronze Age. But by the fourth century B.C. in Hopei as in the other central provinces the normal grave was the rectangular earth with the body laid extended on its back. At other sites near T'ang Shan these have been found with traces of a wooden coffin. Weapons and ornaments were placed inside the coffins, and vessels in the space left outside at the end of the pit, at the feet or head of the occupant. Some graves held double wooden coffins, with a space between the outer and inner to receive the grave-goods. A few of the skeletons were crouched. The practice of burying a dog at the base had ceased.

The pit graves of the middle Chou cemeteries are as a rule not more than 2 or 3 metres long and 1 or 2 metres wide. Their comparatively shallow depth of 2–4 metres has seldom proved sufficient to preserve more than slight traces of the wooden coffins. In the fourth century B.C. graves of this type spread from the central provinces farther to the east and south, Kiangsu and Hunan, and as far west as Szechwan. The numerous tombs of this kind found near Ch'ang Sha in Honan, as much by their structure as their contents are a measure of the growing sinicisation of the Ch'u state. The damp soil in which they are excavated has preserved their timbers in remarkably good condition. The elaborate design of the burial chamber sur- passes any tombs of comparable size in the Central Plain. The scale and finish of the timbers and the precision of their rabbeted jointing may be judged from the example illustrated in Fig. 33. The chamber has double walls, between which the grave-goods of pottery, bronze and lacquer vessels and bronze weapons were laid. The outer and inner coffins, fitted closely together, contained the skeleton laid on its back, with jade *pi* rings at shoulders and knees. The bottom of the burial chamber lay 7 metres below the surface. This depth and the stout timber roofs preserved these tombs from spoliation until recent years, and since 1950 careful excavation has recovered the contents intact from many of them.

Fig. 33

Fig. 32

Most impressive of all the late Chou tombs are those ex-cavated in 1951–5 near Hui Hsien in central Honan. At the village of Liu Li Ko was discovered a group of twenty-seven intact tombs with lacquered coffins, belonging to the late fifth or early fourth centuries B.C. Near to those was a pit con-taining chariots, presumably related to a larger tomb as yet un-discovered, or possibly one already destroyed by treasure-seekers; and a few miles away, near the village of Ku Wei Ts'un, three great tombs were sited in a row east to west. The most elaborate internal structure was found in the middle tomb, No. 2, whose dimensions exceeded even those of a royal tomb of Shang. The plan is a modified version of that seen at Hsin Ts'un: access ramps slope down to the central pit from north and south, the latter—the ceremonial entrance—being con-siderably wider and longer. The total length from north to south was over 200 metres. The upper part of the filling and the

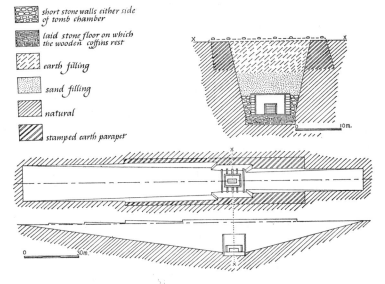

short stone walls either side of tomb chamber

laid stone floor on which the wooden coffins rest

earth filling

sand filling

natural

stamped earth parapet

Fig. 32 Plan and elevations of the great tomb at Ku Wei Ts'un. Hu Hsien, Honan

pit walls were constructed of rammed earth. The timber-built burial chamber rested on a bed of stone slabs and was surrounded by a free stone wall. Soil filled the space between the inner and the outer coffins, and the lower part of the filling over the burial chamber consisted of pure sand

A feature of this tomb unparalleled elsewhere is the capping of a half-metre thick layer laid on the surface over the burial chamber, forming a rectangle of 25 by 6 metres. The border of boulders laid at intervals along the edge of this low platform is the only example so far discovered of an external structure indicating a tomb earlier than the Han dynasty, when mounds were sometimes raised over subterranean brick-built chambers. The setting of stones is reminiscent of the circles built around Bronze Age graves in southern Siberia. The main contents of the Ku Wei Ts'un tombs had been pillaged long before they were excavated. Nevertheless many small bronzes and iron tools which remained, and a jade pendant and a silver-gilt belt-hook which the plunderers had overlooked, are among the finest objects ever recovered in a controlled excavation.

Plate 59

During the first half of the Chou period (Western Chou, 1077–771 B.C.) the armament of the feudal states remained little altered from that of the Shang age. From the tenth century B.C. the *ko* halberd was gradually modified. The base which lay against the haft was lengthened, the inner edge of the blade thus acquiring a concave curve. Eventually a slender and very elegant shape was reached as seen in tombs of the fifth and fourth centuries B.C. Sometimes a spearhead and a halberd blade were combined on a single haft. In examples of the Western Chou period this weapon might be cast in a single piece. Occasionally spearheads and *ko* lie close together in a tomb in positions which suggest that they were hafted together; and in tomb wall-paintings and reliefs of the Han dynasty the composite weapon is seen in the hands of palace guards, by this time being made of iron.

ARMS AND
THE
CHARIOT
Fig. 38

Plate 46

Fig. 39

In a grave of the late fourth or early third century B.C. at Ch'ang Sha in Hunan was discovered the earliest surviving example of the bow. In Fig. 33 it can be seen lying on the north side of the tomb between the inner and outer coffins. Its length of 55 in. is approximately the same as that inferred for the Shang bows, and it is similarly double-curved. Its construction agrees with the description preserved in the Chou Li. The middle part, which extends about two thirds of the length, consists of a core of four plates of bamboo, to which tapering ends are closely fitted and bound on. The whole is bound and glued with bamboo strips and finished with close binding of lacquered silk. Separate wooden tips are notched to receive the cord. The arrowheads of this time are descended from the Shang type, but their trailing barbs are usually longer, the outline often ogival and the central spine less prominent.

From the late fourth century, however, another kind of bronze point is found. They are designed to project little if at all beyond the line of the shaft behind them. Some have a triangular section, with three narrow blades, others are bladeless points, round in section and with blunt rounded heads. Such

Fig. 34

points armed the bolts of the cross-bow. This weapon, evidently a Chinese invention, for it is not known elsewhere at this early date, had a stock and bow of wood, and a trigger mechanism of bronze. It was the principal arm of the soldiers who manned the walls which began to rise in the fourth century B.C. against the incursions of nomads from Inner Mongolia. The power and rapid action of the cross-bow were probably sufficient to keep nomad horsemen at a distance greater than the effective range of the normal bow which they carried. The combination of the cross-bow, the barrier offered by the walls, and the rapid communication along them gave great advantage to a defence which relied on infantry conscripts. The northern boundary states of Ch'in, Chao and Yen had already built long sections of wall in the second half of the

1 lacquered shield

2,3 lacquered wine-cups

4–6 bronze vessels

7–9 pottery vessels

10 lacquered dish

11,12 wooden grave attendants

13 wooden sword

14 wooden spear

15 wooden grave attendant

16 fragments of a wooden bamboo basket

17 mechanism of a cross-bow

18 bow with its string

19 halberd

20,21 fragments of leather bags

22 bamboo model of a boat

23 lacquered table

24 lacquered toilet box

25 bronze sword

26 pottery censer

27 bronze sword

28–33 jade rings, pi

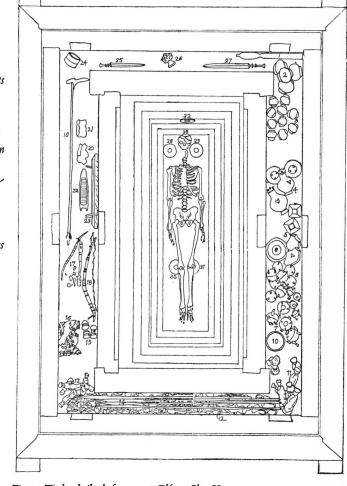

Fig. 33 Timber-built shaft-grave at Ch'ang Sha, Hunan. 4th-3rd century B.C. The grave gifts are placed between the multiple coffin and the outer walls of the burial chamber. Scale approx. 1:36

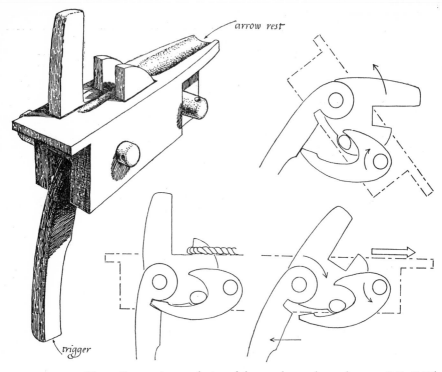

Fig. 34 Bronze trigger-mechanism of the cross-bow. 3rd or 2nd century B.C. British Museum. Length: 11 cm.

fourth and the early third centuries B.C. Shih Huang Ti rebuilt and completed the line. His Myriad League Great Wall remains today substantially the same in fabric, though repaired in parts from time to time down to the Ming period. For the historian this astounding monument symbolises the end of feudalism and the foundation of the united empire. Its length is over 2500 miles, stretching from the coast of the Po Hai opposite the Liao T'ung peninsula to Yang Kuan just beyond the western tip of Kansu province.

The chariot retained its military importance in the Chou period, though probably its usefulness declined in the last few centuries when battles were increasingly fought by vast armies of conscripted infantry, and no longer by the charioteer patrician with his following of retainers. But even then the number of chariots a feudal prince could command was a measure of his strength. For Confucius and Mencius a power, ful ruler is a 'prince of ten thousand chariots'.

Museum collections include many axle-caps with linch pin (the only indispensable metal part of the chariot), which can be dated to the early and middle Chou centuries from the style of their decoration; but from the beginning of the Chou period until about 700 B.C. evidence for the structure of the vehicle is very slight. Chariots might still be buried in the funerals of the great, as at Chang Chia Pa in Shensi, where a chariot with four horses and another with two horses had been placed in a single pit. A tomb near the eastern suburb of Loyang, much disturbed by grave-robbers, contained the wheels of five chariots, and a pit near-by held eight horses. The wheels here have 20–24 spokes, and the shape of the box, to judge from the trace of its base, is similar to that of the Shang chariot. The axle-caps have ornament which places them about 800 B.C.

Plate 39

Fig. 46

The chariots of the middle Chou period can be reconstructed in considerable detail from the results of brilliant excavations made in Honan province. One of these was the chariot-pit at Hui Hsien mentioned on p. 32 where Mr Hsia Nai and his colleagues of the Institute of Archaeology revealed entire casts of nineteen chariots by tracing the deposit of fine, compact earth which had replaced the long-vanished timbers, a feat of excavation comparable only to the recovery of the 'ghost' of the ship-burial at Sutton Hoo in East Anglia in 1939. In 1956–7 another chariot-pit was excavated in the same way at Shang Ts'un Ling on the Yellow river in east Honan, and proved to contain eleven chariots of which five were revealed intact. In this tomb two bronze halberds were inscribed with the

Plate 52
Fig. 35

name 'Prince-heir Yüan T'u of Kuo', and a bronze *li* was marked 'Tzŭ Tso of the Chi family of Kuo'. According to the *Tso Chuan* the state of Kuo was annexed by the state of Chin in 655 B.C., and it is presumed that the tombs as a whole belong to the eighth to early seventh centuries B.C. This date is sup-ported by the shapes and decoration of the numerous ritual vessels of bronze which accompanied the burials. The chariots of Hui Hsien are separated from those of Shang Ts'un Ling by more than two centuries, but the vehicles of the two groups are almost identical in construction.

At Hui Hsien, where the arrangement of the burial is better preserved, the nineteen chariots were closely packed in two rows facing east in a pit measuring 21 metres by 7·8 metres and 4·4 metres deep. The shaft of each rested on the box of the chariot in front. A narrow balk of earth separated off a section 3 metres in length at the east end. Of this compartment only a small part had been spared by the builders of a Han tomb which intruded on the pit. Even in so small a space forty-four horses had been heaped. In nearly every case the shapes of the chariot parts were preserved in the earth. The reconstruction shows a vehicle differing little in essentials from the Shang chariot. The lacquer paint which had covered the rails around the box left enough trace to suggest their size and form with fair accuracy. The sides of the driver's platform were better preserved, however, at Shang Ts'un Ling: the box was 1·3 metres wide, reaching to the hubs on either side, and only 85 cm. deep from back to front. It was surrounded by railings only 30 cm. high formed of spaced upright and horizontal wooden rods, a gap being left in the centre of the back for mounting.

All but a few of the chariot bronzes (which in addition to axle-caps and jingles from the yoke included finials from the rails) had been removed before burial at Hui Hsien. The 26-spoked wheels, finer than those of Shang or Western Chou,

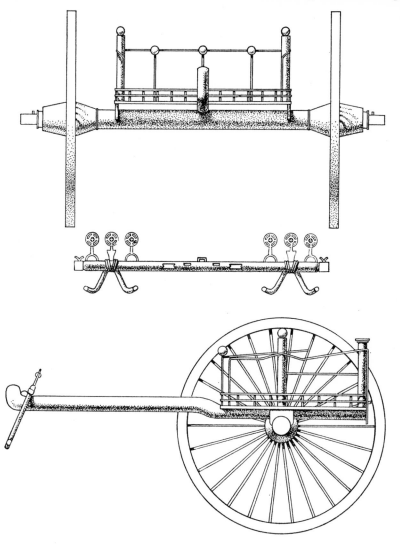

Fig. 35 Reconstruction of chariot from excavations at Liu Li Ko, Hui Hsien, Honan. 4th century B.C. The axle caps and the ornaments of the yoke and of the rear pillars of the box are of bronze. Scale 1:20

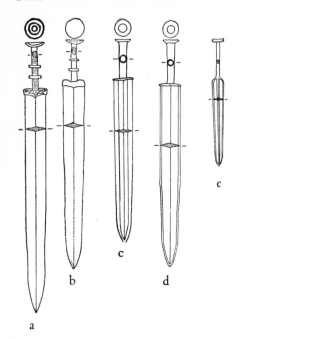

Fig. 36 Bronze swords: a, from Shang Ts'un Ling, Late 8th or early 7th century B.C., b-e: from Chung Chou Lu, Loyang 6th-4th centuries, B.C. Scale approx. 1:6

Fig. 37 Bronze sword with hand-and-serpent mark. South-west China. 4th-3rd century B.C. Scale 1:3

still depended on pegging or lashing, for no bronze parts appeared with them. Some of the wheels are 'dished', having their rims advanced outwards beyond the plane in which the spokes enter the hub, and are strengthened by two parallel struts set across them near the diameter. These chariots presumably entered the pit on the completion of the funeral procession, and their horses were slaughtered and consigned to the annex prepared for them at one end of the chariot-pit. No trace remains here to throw light on the method of harness. The form of yoke suggests that it was still of the choker type descended from Shang: even so light a chariot still called for two horses. But the linked bronze bridle-bits which were found in the chariot-pit at Shang Ts'un Ling and in a smaller grave at Hui Hsien are a new device.

A strange feature of the armament of the earlier feudal period is the lack of a sword, which does not appear until the later sixth century B.C. Thereafter swords are common in tombs through central China from Shensi to Hunan. It is probable, as has been often argued, that the Chinese sword is a borrowing from the nomads of the steppes, who at this period were already armed with their *akinakes*, but from the start the Chinese sword is quite different. The hilt is cast in one piece with the blade, and either tubular or formed of a solid thin stem with two ring-like swellings at the centre. On some pieces preserved at Ch'ang Sha with their wooden sheaths we may see the binding of cord which completed the grip. Normally the blade is of narrow rhomboid section, and two thirds down the length it is slightly narrowed to give an outline like that of the 'carp's tongue' swords of the late Bronze Age of Europe.

Hardly any development can be traced in the shape of these swords. The type with ringed grip may have been adopted a little later than the one with a tubular handle, and it is the only form found in the late fourth- and third-century graves; but the two types were in use together for a time. A few swords are known which have a simple hafting spike, but their date is not clear, and there is nothing to show that they were the forerunners of the swords with cast handles.[5] A more likely ancestor of these is the form of dagger found at Shang Ts'un Ling: it looks like a narrow spearhead with prominent central rib and rounded shoulders, to which is added a plain thin handle ending in a disc pommel. Its length is only 14 in. If daggers of this kind existed when the Chinese adopted the sword in imitation of the nomads, it is understandable that they should not have copied the nomads' weapon exactly.

Plates 48, 49

Fig. 36

Plate 50

Fig. 37

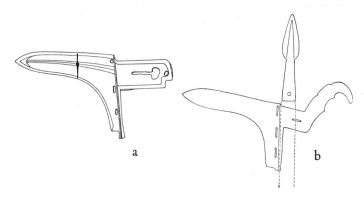

Fig. 38 Bronze halberds: a, from Liu Li Ko, Hui Hsien, Honan; b, from Chung Chou Lu, near Loyang, Honan: The spearhead and halberd had been mounted on the same haft. 5th-4th century B.C. Scale 1:4

The shortness of the Chinese swords can hardly have been determined merely by the relation of weight and rigidity. The short sword looks like a horseman's weapon, made to sling conveniently from the belt when its owner is in the saddle. Such swords are worn in this way by the horsemen depicted in the bronze figurines from Shih Chai Shan in Szechwan.

The adoption of the sword must mark an important change in methods of warfare, and one connected with frontier defence against the nomads in the north-west. Towards the end of the fifth century B.C. the northern boundary state of Chao adopted cavalry, imitating its enemies, the nomadic Turkish and Mongol tribes whose mounted razzias were proving so costly. Hitherto cavalry had not been used in Chinese armies, familiar with horses though they were for chariots. The other northern states, and especially Ch'in, copied Chao's example.

IRON The further history of Chinese swords involves the still obscure question of the rise and spread of iron metallurgy. When it is buried in damp soil iron resists corrosion much less than bronze, and it is not surprising that the unlovely rusted objects and fragments were discarded by excavators who sought only bronzes for the antique market. Before the war iron objects of late-Chou date had been discovered in systematic excavation only in the north-eastern provinces of Liao Ning and Hopei. Recently they have been found at sites in Honan and Shensi; and, far from the ancient seats of Chinese culture, in territory to which little of the metropolitan Chinese culture had spread before 500 B.C., at Ch'ang Sha in Hunan and in Szechwan.

The most varied iron tools were found in the Hui Hsien tombs. They comprise edges for the square and pointed blades of wooden spades; narrower spade blades made wholly of the metal and socketed to receive wooden handles; edging for an axe-blade and a few specimens of the socketed axe which, in bronze, had continued to be made almost unaltered since Shang times. Other sites have produced broad and narrow iron hoes with strong hafting sockets set at right angles to the blades, and rectangular and crescentic sickles. Nearly all of these are clearly agricultural tools. Only the socketed spade and axe have an ancestry in bronze forms of earlier times. The digging tools are designed to reinforce wooden blades, or copy the shape of a wooden hoe. The sickles reproduce the stone knives which first appear in the Neolithic period.

From these iron tools we can infer something of the conditions of agriculture in the earlier Chou centuries. As in the rest of the world, the high cost of bronze, the difficulty of working it and the interest which rulers had in preserving a monopoly of bronze as the material of weapons and a substance of wealth, prevented the spread of this metal among the peasantry. Farmers worked their comparatively light soil with wooden spades and hoes which were improved versions of the digging sticks of the most primitive agriculturalists. The long survival of stone reaping-knives (they are said to have been found in use in remote regions in recent times) and their direct translation into iron

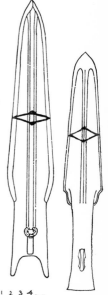

Fig. 39 Bronze spear-heads. From Chung Chou Lu, Loyang. 5th-3rd centuries, B.C. Scale 2:9

when this became available is striking proof of the denial of bronze to the farmers: bronze evidently could not be had even for their most essential cutting tool.

Fig. 40

The iron tools from the Hui Hsien tombs are skilful castings, and we must assume that long experience of iron founding lies behind them. Although archaeology has not yet given proof of the use of iron at an earlier date, references to iron in literature are sure evidence of the knowledge of it before 500 B.C. In general the literary evidence is held to support the introduction of iron in the seventh or sixth centuries. The only early closelydated allusion, in the *Tso Chuan*, speaks of the casting of iron cauldrons (*ting*) in 512 B.C., when a minister of the state of Chin levied from the people more than a quarter of a ton for this purpose. On the vessels were inscribed penal laws. This is skilled founding, and we must suppose that iron had already been known for some time. Iron moulds for casting socketed axes, found at Hsing Lung Hsien in Lehol province, can hardly be later than the 6th century.

Some bronze spades of Shang age can be brought into the argument about the date of the introduction of iron. They are known from tombs at Loyang and near Hsiao T'un (Ta Ssŭ K'ung), where, like the Hui Hsien spades, they may have been ritually buried after serving to dig the funeral pit. The shape, with socket of oblong rectangular section and, generally, rounded shoulders, comes very close to the iron specimens made some six centuries later. Moreover, a spade blade of the Shang type was the model for the earliest Chinese bronze currency, which circulated in the region between south Shensi and south Hopei. On admittedly slight evidence numismatists date the circulation of these spade coins in the late eighth and the seventh centuries B.C. They point out that it is improbable in China, any more than in other parts of the world, that a bronze currency should have circulated before iron was known and while bronze was the only industrial metal.

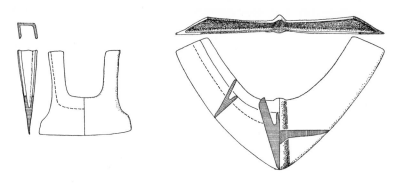

Fig. 40 Iron edges for axe and spade. From Ku Wei Ts'un, Hui Hsien. Scale 1:4

But even if we accept a later date for the issue of the spade money, nearer to 600 B.C., a problem remains. No specimens are known which would link the Shang bronze spade of the twelfth or eleventh centuries B.C. to its parallel in iron in the fifth or fourth centuries. It still seems improbable that iron forms should fill the gap before 600. Two somewhat unlikely hypo-theses remain: that the resemblance of a carefully designed shape at two remote times is accidental, or that both versions copied wooden forms of which naturally no trace survives. But the resemblance seems too close for chance, and the spade socket can hardly ever have been made of wood. Another obscure question which we may look to the iron implements to answer is the date of the earliest use of draught animals in tillage. The Chou tribes are sometimes said to have introduced them when they moved westwards to the conquest of the Shang. But archaeology remains silent on this matter until, possibly, the discovery of the Hui Hsien tools which we have described; for here the larger iron edge of V-section shaped to reinforce a broadly pointed blade may have been part of a plough-share, and not merely a spade. But, in both senses, it is flimsy evidence. We infer from the histories that the water buffalo, the draught animal of rice-cultivating communities, was already widely used in south and central China in the second half of the Chou period. Its domestication, like the development of rice cultivation itself, must have taken place in the south.

In weapons the replacement of bronze by iron was a slower process in China than in Europe. In the West iron was adopted for swords, daggers and spears as soon as the art of working it was mastered. In China the majority of such weapons were made of bronze until the third century B.C., long after iron was in use for tools of the kind found at Hui Hsien. This situation is reflected in a remark attributed to the philosopher Kuan Tzŭ in an improving conversation with Duke Huan of Ch'i:

'The lovely metal (i.e. bronze) is used for casting of swords and pikes, it is used in company of dogs and horses (i.e. for profitless hunting). The ugly metal (i.e. iron) is used for casting of hoes which flatten (weeds) and axes which fell (trees). It is used upon the fruitful earth.'[6]

The reason for the lateness of iron weapons lies in a peculiarity of Chinese methods. The development of iron technology reverses the sequence followed in Europe, and hitherto assumed to be the natural one: the Chinese cast iron from the start, and, as far as we can tell at present, did not forge it till two or three centuries later. In Europe forging was the original process, and the only one practised for two thousand years, until the discovery of casting in the fourteenth century A.D. The skill of the Chinese iron-casters of the feudal period may be judged from the clean, strong lines of the Hui Hsien iron tools. It is even more striking in the high quality of the iron casting moulds excavated from a foundry site at Hsing Lung in Jehol province. Eighty-seven moulds for hoes, spades, sickles, chisels, chariot parts and axes were recovered, and the form of the last indicated a date not later than the fourth century B.C.

Plate 51

A mile to the west of the site are traces of an ancient mine from which the ore could be obtained. But cast iron is unsuitable for thin, sharp edges and points. So long as casting was the only method of working the new metal, swords must still be made of bronze. Only forged iron could supply superior arms and affect the warfare of the states.

The evidence of a dozen sites where iron objects were found, spread over north and central China from Shensi to Hopei, suggests that only casting was known in this region before the end of the Chou period.[7] Agricultural tools of the types we have already described, chisels and belt hooks have been recorded, but no iron swords or even knives. The only iron parts that must have been forged are the tangs of arrowheads, of which the point itself is made of bronze. These have been found at Hsia Tu, the capital of the state of Yen in Hopei, at Cheng Chou in Honan and at Tou Chi T'ai in Shensi.

In Hunan, on the other hand, in ancient territory of the Ch'u state, forging was known earlier. In a tomb at Ch'ang Sha an iron dagger was found together with a form of pottery *li* which suggests a date not later than *c.* 400 B.C.:[8] iron was known here little if at all later than in the central states. Sixty-four Ch'u graves of the fourth to early third centuries at Ch'ang Sha and Heng Yang produced a total of over seventy iron objects, of which thirty-three were weapons, including swords, *chi* (the combined spear and halberd), daggers, knives and spearheads. In the manufacture of these the iron can only have been forged.[9] The possession of the iron sword would have given the Ch'u armies a decided advantage over enemies still fighting with the bronze sword, and would help to explain the success of Ch'u arms and the expansion of the Ch'u state in the fourth century B.C. But the superiority of the iron sword, its greater length and resilience and better edge, seem not to have ousted the bronze weapon. In a large group of Ch'u graves at Ch'ang Sha excavated more recently by the Institute

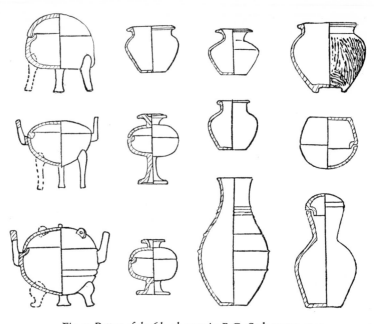

Fig. 41 Pottery of the 6th-4th centuries B.C. Scale approx. 1:14

of Archaeology only the short 'classical' bronze sword, and bronze *ko* and spearheads of the standard types were found.

Archaeology can yet give little support to the theory that the possession of the iron sword was the decisive factor in the suc- cess of the Ch'in conquest. But Ch'in was able to exploit iron ores in Szechwan province, and the rapid and universal adoption of iron arms about the time of the unification sug- gests that Ch'in was chiefly responsible for the change. The histories frequently relate the ferocity of the Ch'in armies in beheading their enemies by the thousand, a prowess perhaps reflecting the superior swordsmanship conferred by the iron weapon.[10] The iron swords of Han times are of two types. One is two-edged, about an inch and a quarter wide at the guard and tapering only slightly to the point, with a hafting tang on which guard and pommel, sometimes of bronze or jade, were fitted separately. The other sword has a single-edge, and a still narrower blade. Its cast-on ring handle gives it the appearance of an enlarged version of a form of knife made by the nomads of the north-west: here is possibly a reflexion of the part Ch'in played in propagating the iron sword.

The spread of cast iron tools in the sixth to fourth centuries B.C. initiated a revolution in agricultural methods, facilitating tillage and irrigation and increasing the production of food. It also gave rise to an industrial class whose activities were a chief topic with economists. History records the growth and wealth of this class, and clearly it caused anxiety to the government, which was still inclined to attempt to control the producers of iron. Of the methods of these iron-masters we still know very little. The analysis of the ancient iron has only recently been taken in hand. It is uncertain whether forging was a method of working iron already extracted and cast, or arose directly from the treatment of particularly rich ores. Furnace bellows were employed by Han times, at the latest. Any light which archaeologists are able in the future to throw on the earlier history of iron technology may add to our knowledge of the political history of China, particularly the reasons for the military power of the Ch'u and Ch'in states.

CHAPTER IV

The Art of the Bronze Age

IN ART AS IN OTHER MATTERS China is a country extraordinarily tenacious of tradition. Some themes invented over three millennia ago, at the beginning of the Bronze Age, are still meaningful in Chinese eyes. As ornament in por, celain, lacquer and jade the motifs are now banal enough. But in the forms in which they first appeared and while they con, tinued to dominate the whole visual art through the Shang dynasty and the earlier Chou dynasty they have a power still capable of stirring our imagination.

The Bronze Age tradition was submerged for a thousand years after the close of the Chou dynasty. The arts of Han, of the period of the Six Dynasties and of the T'ang Dynasty take a quite different course, and one less estranging to the occidental whose heritage is the naturalistic art of Greece and Rome. Throughout this period there are recorded instances of the interest Chinese antiquaries took in the relics of Shang and Chou. By the Sung period we can speak of an archaistic revival in art which accompanied a renewed interest in the Confucian philosophy and ancient epigraphy. Sung porcelain copied the shapes of the ancient ritual vessels. In Ming and Ch'ing times motifs from the decoration of the ancient bronzes were copied and adapted in bronze, jade, and lacquer, supplying ornament of a dry, dignified kind, to our eyes perhaps unexciting, but seldom sinking into banality. The courtly, overloaded decora, tive schemes of Ch'ing art were the basis of the European *chinoiserie*. The ornament which charmed the rococo taste in the West touches at some points a tradition which leads back to the vision of Shang and Chou artists.

As it has been preserved for us, Bronze Age art is largely the art of the bronze-worker, and its development is traced in

the ornament which he applied to vessels, weapons and utilitarian objects with surpassing skill. It is predominantly a two-
dimensional art, delighting in vital linear figures subordinated
strictly and appropriately to the forms on which they appear.
Sculpture on a large scale was never attempted, and of painting
—other than linear pattern allied to the bronze ornament—
only a single example, of the third century B.C., has survived
burial. On a small scale, as additional decoration of ornate
bronze vessels, plastic figures of animals abound, though
similar portrayals of the human figure are rare.

In the decoration of bronze vessels excavated at Cheng Chou
(Pai Chia Chuang site, Shang III) the art of the earlier Shang
period has already a sophisticated air, as if it had a long development behind it. It deals already with conventional formulas:
in the neck of the vessels an animal mask with prominent eyes
appears at the centre of a band of pattern which has no obvious
connexion with natural or even simple geometric forms. The
origin of this style of decoration is obscure. Its character does
not suggest that it was invented for casting on bronze in the
first place, but hints rather at an earlier development in carved
wood or bone. Unfortunately such perishable material has not
survived from the Neolithic to illustrate the possible ancestry
of Bronze Age art. The schematised face painted on a pot
found at the Yang Shao village at Pan P'o Ts'un (p. 39 above)   Plate 5
is the only possible neolithic link with a bronze motif—the
ubiquitous animal mask—and the connexion is not very
convincing. The spirals and other figures painted on Kansu
neolithic urns and the motifs found on painted pottery in the
Central Plain are alike remote from the artistic ideas of the
Bronze Age. In the Lung Shan Neolithic culture there is
nothing of artistic import which leads on to the Shang dynasty.
Nevertheless it seems likely that some elements of Shang art
existed before the acquisition of metallurgical knowledge and
the dawn of the Bronze Age; and that ornament previously

carved in wood and bone and already elaborate and refined was then transmuted into metal. The same phenomenon occurs later, when new styles of equally sophisticated bronze orna/ ment appear suddenly in southern regions to which the mastery of bronze had just penetrated.

The earliest phase of Bronze Age art, that of the Shang state, is at home in Honan province. Although we know it best in bronze, enough of other materials survive to show that the repertoire of designs used by the bronze/caster was not con/ fined to his craft alone. The same style pervaded work done in wood, ivory, jade, stone and the white pottery, and was applied indifferently to ritual vessels, weapons, axes, chariot parts and personal ornaments. It is an 'animal art', in which the main motifs are taken from the shapes of animals, real or imaginary. It differs fundamentally, however, from the later art of the Scyths and the other steppe nomads. This copies parts of real animals faithfully, then combines them into a fantastic whole, joining birds' heads to tiger/like bodies, adding extra heads and strange crests and horns. But the dragons and monster/masks of Shang art are divorced from reality, reduced from the start to abstract symmetry and often rendered in a bewildering pat/ tern of hooked and scrolled lines which loses nearly all contact with organic forms.

Plate 19

For all the complexity of the designs, the ornament comprises a comparatively small number of motifs. The monster/mask called *t'ao t'ieh* is commonest of all, and is chiefly responsible for the disquieting effect of much of the bronze décor. Its origin and the reasons for its strange anatomy have not been explained. Perhaps they were no better accounted for by the Shang them/ selves than they are in the moralising interpolations of later times when it was said to be a warning against greed. The mask is a distillation of feline ferocity. It lacks the lower jaw in all but a few examples, and huge fangs protrude from the upper one. In the less abstracted designs a lozenge/shaped

Fig. 42a

figure is placed on the nose-ridge between the eyes. The latter are round or slightly elongated horizontally and always protrude above the general level of the relief. The nose-ridge ends above in a crest of varying form and either side of this are horns, which may be shaped like eyebrows into recumbent Cs, or are curved upwards and inwards. In the more intelligible forms patterned bands extend sideways from the region of the eyes, to terminate with an upward scroll which is regarded as the *t'ao t'ieh's* tail. Beneath these bands, either side of the upper jaw, are claws consisting of a number of hooks. The doubling of the body at either side of the face in *t'ao t'ieh* and serpents depicted on the bronzes simply follows the requirements of symmetry and frontal posture.

a

b

Fig. 42 a, T'ao T'ieh *and b,* k'uei. *Later Shang period. 14th-11th centuries, B.C.*

Next to the *t'ao t'ieh*, the commonest figure of the ornament is a creature which from Sung times has been termed a dragon. This is not the familiar whiskered dragon of medieval and later Chinese art, but the *k'uei*, which is spoken of in some pre-Han texts and which mythology connects with rain-making. In the Shang version it appears always in side view, extending a single paw beneath its gaping jaws. Perhaps it was this presentation in profile that gave rise to the belief that it possessed only one leg. Its chief variants are classified by Karlgren as trunked, beaked, jawed, turning, feathered, winged. It is never reduced, like the *t'ao t'ieh*, to a maze of lines, nor is it ever confused with the snake, which in its rarer appearances remains quite distinct. Although it is generally placed horizontally, the dragon also stands on its head either side of a *tao t'ieh* mask. It is in connexion with the mask that its nature is most mysterious. The ridge which usually runs down the middle of the *t'ao t'ieh* often divides the design into halves, each of which forms a *k'uei* exactly similar to *k'uei* used independently in the ornament. When the vertical *k'uei* flank a *t'ao t'ieh* they take the place of the lateral developments of the mask design. In either case it looks as if the *k'uei* arose from the fanciful treatment of the mask: starting from a more or less realistic design this may have disintegrated into separate elements as time went on. But it has also been suggested that it was the confrontation of two *k'uei* which led to the *t'ao t'ieh*. Another theory, advanced by Loehr when he attempted to relate the patterns of the painted neolithic pottery to the bronze décor, is that the mask began with an eye amid a maze of spirals, around which a face eventually coalesced, becoming a logical unit of eyes, ears, horns and jaws, and finally, disintegrating again, reverted to more or less abstract pattern in which these elements were separated or lost from sight. Proof or disproof of any of these theories would require much more dated material than we at present possess, and it is possible that they all err in supposing that the designs developed in clear successive steps. We can only note that the Cheng Chou motifs are already dissolved into linear patterns, while more 'naturalistic' *t'ao t'ieh* come from Hsiao T'un and are later in date.

The *t'ao t'ieh* set at the centre of a band of linear pattern as found at Cheng Chou and Hui Hsien is the only style of bronze ornament which we can attribute so far to the pre-Hsiao-T'un period. There is no doubt that at least during the latter part of the occupation of the northern capital the repertoire of ornament and the skill available to render it in metal had greatly increased. An innovation at Hsiao T'un was to combine the masks and dragons with small geometric figures. Spirals and hooks in engraved line cover the raised portions of the main elements and the whole is set on a ground of small, tight spirals of circular and squared shape, the 'thunder pattern', so named from its resemblance to a character of the script. The effect gives a restless confined movement to the design, like the squirming of the cilia of an elementary sea-creature. Plate 20

Some simpler schemes found at Hsiao T'un come close to the Cheng Chou style, the friezes of ornament being rendered either in thin raised line or in a line which has the appearance of being engraved on a flat surface. But on nobler vessels this ornament is refined, repeated and elaborated to cover the whole available surface, set in horizontal bands and divided vertically by prominent flanges, the deeper of which have rows of T-shaped cuts just failing to penetrate their thickness. The 'thunder pattern' is an addition to this evolved décor, and is never found with the simpler designs. At the same time, as the *horror vacui* seizes the draughtsmen, they introduce zigzags, rhomboi and scale patterns. The final stage in the logical development of the ornament seems to be reached when parts of the designs are raised in high relief, sometimes in relief at two levels, when horns and ears project into space, and whole vessels may be made in the shapes of animals.

This rich style must have matured in the later part of the Hsiao T'un period, perhaps not before the end of the twelfth century B.C. It is vessels so decorated that bear inscriptions occasionally. The carved ornament of the fine white pottery corresponds to this style with only such differences as the different material would account for. Stylised birds, snakes and cicadas are included in the bronze decoration, while entire vessels take the shapes of rams, elephants and owls. But the field in which the draughtsmen could experiment was still strictly limited. If we discern magical intent in the swathing of sacred vessels in monster masks and dragons—and that conclusion seems inescapable—we may imagine the craftsman conforming to superstitious custom. Beginning with the ornament of ritual vessels, this narrow but powerful convention dominated no less in the embellishment of weapons and utilitarian objects. The formal and dramatic potentialities of the few conventions were exploited more intensively than was ever done in similar circumstances elsewhere in the ancient world, whether in Egypt, Greece of the Geometric Age, or the Maya and Aztec cultures of Central America which the Shang approaches most closely in spirit. The great bronze vessels of the last decades of the Shang dynasty seem to culminate the quest for an arresting symbol of the magical rite of sacrifice.

Certain designs used in Shang bronze art resisted the dismemberment which was apt to overtake the *t'ao t'ieh*, and to a lesser extent the *k'uei* dragon. The intact and comparatively naturalistic bovine masks, the deer mask as found on a famous *ting* excavated at Hsiao T'un, rams' heads such as those on the great *tsun* in the British Museum, the elephants and owls formed into vessels, were probably all acceptable as representing animals which were slaughtered in the royal sacrifices.

The manner in which the motifs are combined shows interesting divergencies. In his division of the motifs of Shang art into three categories, Karlgren places together the bovine

Plate 30

Plate 14
Plate 15

Fig. 43 Jade amulets. Later Shang period. 14th-11th centuries B.C. British Museum. Scale 2:3

mask, intact *t'ao t'ieh*, *t'ao t'ieh* with a coherent 'body', cicada and vertical *k'uei*. These motifs are combined into all-over ornament which is free of the tendency to linear elaboration and dissolution. The 'dissolved' *t'ao t'ieh*, a form of bird in which the tail has become separated from the body, and repetitive minor geometrical figures associated with these, are never combined with motifs taken from the first group. A third list, comprising the less abstracted *t'ao t'ieh*, the varieties of horizontal *k'uei*, the intact bird and another series of geometric figures, makes use of motifs which appear combined indifferently with

Fig. 47

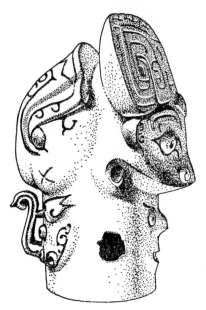

Fig. 44 Bronze pole finial. Later Shang period. 12th-11th century B.C. British Museum. Scale 1:2

elements belonging to either of the two other groups. From this Karlgren argues that the first group, with its more coherent forms and greater plasticity, represents a style of earlier date than that which made use of motifs belonging to the second group, though the two may have overlapped for a time. This conclusion has not been generally accepted; the evidence from Cheng Chou, as we have seen, tends to disprove it. It is possible, as an alternative explanation, that the more naturalistic and the 'dissolved' styles of ornament were the work of artists attached to different bronze foundries.

No less than the creators of the later animal art of the steppe nomads of central Asia, the Shang artist could observe animals sympathetically and portray them with unaffected naturalism, whenever the conventions of the ornamental style might be laid aside. Such subjects as the side view of deer with reverted heads on a wine bucket (yu),[1] profiles of Przewalski's steppe horse in the emblems cast on bronze[2] and of deer, hare and birds among the small jade amulet plaques, are sensitively drawn without decorative bias. The realism and expression of the head, and the stance of a zoomorphic vessel can create a vivid illusion of life even when the form as a whole is fantastic. These are hints of a naturalistic art practised alongside the hieratic convention proper to the sacral bronzes and funeral gifts which have come down to us. The hieratic style is fundamentally Chinese, too specialised in its forms and application to have had any influence beyond the Yellow river valley to the north and west. But the naturalistic animal art belongs to a wider tradition. Some of its most striking products at Hsiao T'un were the horse and ibex heads decorating the handles of the bronze knives found in the graves of the later period. These, as we have seen, are links with the Bronze Age of southern Siberia, both in the form of the knife and the style of the animal ornament. We cannot be certain in which direction the artistic influence passed between Siberia and China. Future research may solve the problem by revealing something of the bronze culture of north Shensi and Kansu, i.e. the intermediate territory, during Shang times.

Plate 27
Fig. 44

Fig. 21a

The artistic traditions no less than the political state of the Shang were due to be overthrown by the Chou conquest of 1027 B.C. Students of the bronze vessels and their inscriptions have paid more attention to the problem of distinguishing late Shang from early Chou than to any other. Since the number of bronzes assured of a Shang date by excavation is small compared with those which survive without documentation, the argument has turned inevitably on intrinsic features and generally on the evidence of inscription. By this means Karlgren demonstrated that many ornamental motifs of the late Shang style survived into the tenth century B.C. Indeed, he seems finally to have despaired of establishing any simple

INNOVATIONS
OF THE
EARLY CHOU
PERIOD

criteria for distinguishing Shang vessels from those of the earliest decades of Chou.

It has often been assumed that the changes seen in the bronze vessels after 1027 B.C. are the result of the inferior taste and technical resources of the new masters corrupting the art bequeathed to them by Shang. But it is more probable that the Chou people were already familiar with monster masks and dragons in their homeland in Shensi, that they shared mythological and artistic traditions broadly with the Shang, even if their art had a distinct local character. Unfortunately excavations have thrown no light on the nature of Chou art before their move eastwards to conquer Shang in 1027 B.C. The earliest inscribed and datable bronze vessel from the western region is a *ho* wine pourer from P'u Tu Ts'un in Shensi which belongs to the reign of King Mu, in the later tenth century B.C. But there are many signs that the Chou brought something of their own into the culture of the Central Plain. In the decoration of the bronze vessels the changes that occur soon after 1027 B.C. are too sudden and too positive to be merely the result of degeneration. The expansion of the bronze inscriptions in the first Chou reigns, their sophisticated language and elegant script, suggest that the Chou scribes were not merely pupils of their Shang predecessors, any more than the designers of the ornament of the Chou bronzes were entirely dependent on what they copied from Shang art. In one case at least, a bronze *kuei* bowl set on a square pedestal in a manner unknown at Hsiao T'un, the phrasing of the inscription makes one strongly suspect that it was cast before Wu Wang's defeat of the Shang.[3]

It is certain that after 1000 B.C. at the latest, if not on the very morrow of the fall of the capital at Hsiao T'un, the graphic and relief bronze décors most characteristic of Shang art fell out of fashion. The most typical and eccentric Shang shapes, the *ku*, *chüeh*, *chia* and the zoomorphic vases, ceased to be made.

The *t'ao t'ieh* dissolved among scrollery becomes rarer. More solid designs are favoured and the outlines are often frilled with rows of hook-like quills not seen before. At times the relief is grotesque, and is concerned more with producing a startling profile than with enlivening the interest of surface ornament. Deep jagged flanges overload some of the shapes. If these were the only innovations, one might speak of Chou art as a bar-barous exaggeration of features present in germ in Shang art. But simultaneously, or very shortly afterwards, there appear other more refined shapes and ornament which do not derive from Hsiao T'un. The *kuei* of the Marquis of Hsing preserved in the British Museum illustrates one of these. The motifs of the décor are depicted in a thin raised and rounded line on a plain ground. The restraint of the ornament and the dignity of the vessel contrast utterly with the plastic extravaganzas of other pieces which must be nearly contemporary.

Plate 34

From the late eleventh century B.C. the tense upward move-ment of the profile characteristic of the Hsiao T'un vessels gives way to heavier more inert shapes with curves spreading in the lower part. The handled *kuei* and the *yu* wine bucket, in which this change in the feeling for form can best be followed, are comparatively rare among vessels known with certainty to have been excavated in or around Hsiao T'un. On the other hand, both figure in a number of tomb sets of sacral vessels thought to be of late Shang date found farther to the south-west in the same province, near Loyang, the place due to be chosen as the eastern capital of the first Chou rulers.[4] Their appearance here is perhaps a cultural sign of the encroachment of the Chou which culminated in the defeat of the Shang king.

Plate 31

The rôle which the Chou rulers assigned to the ritual bronzes in their political ceremonial ensured the dispersal of these throughout the territory which they had brought under their control. The inscribed *kuei* recently found at Yen Tun Shan in Kiangsu testifies at once both to this dispersal and to

Plate 33

the independence of the Chou tradition of bronze craft, for its inscription shows that the vessel was cast in or just after the reign of King Ch'eng at the end of the eleventh or the very beginning of the tenth centuries B.C. *Kuei* of the shape seen at Yen Tun Shan, with high foot, hooked flanges and four heavy handles surmounted by animal heads (the form of these is sometimes reminiscent of a deer head, but they are no more natural than the *t'ao t'ieh*), continued to be made well into the tenth century. Often the bowl was set on a high base or on four low feet. The decoration might still be based on the *t'ao t'ieh* though occasionally a pair of heads with gaping jaws face each other in side view. But before 1000 B.C. a form of con-

Fig. 45 ventionalised bird with long tail and plume invaded the decoration, and in its larger versions was the basis of some of the finest designs of the tenth century.

THE MIDDLE   In the middle and later part of the Western Chou period
CHOU STYLE (*c.* 950–771) the commonest vessels are a new type of *ting* with hemispherical bowl set on bulging curved legs, *kuei* with
Plate 32 lid and large monster-head handles, and a rectangular version of a food container termed *fu*. The decoration is coarser, being often designed in a broad flat band. Rolled and twisted-and-
Fig. 45 rolled dragons of a new kind are popular. For the first time we find schemes of large-scale repetitive figures, geometric, or reminiscent in detail of the dragon pattern. One frequent motif resembles two recumbent Gs set either side of a small boss which seems to be the vestige of an eye. The motifs are developed as geometrical figures in a spirit quite distinct from the more

Fig. 45 Decorative motifs from bronzes. Late 11th-18th centuries B.C.

organic formulas of the older styles. In the light of the later history of Chinese bronze art the rise of the Middle Chou style is even more significant than the replacement of the Shang tradition by the style of the early Chou period.

Where and when the middle Chou style was evolved is uncertain, but the choice must lie between central Honan and southern Shensi. The earliest dated example of the 'recumbent Gs' motif is the decoration of the neck and lid of the *ho* from P'u Tu Ts'un in southern Shensi, which belong to the late tenth century B.C. Many bronze vessels with ornament of sinuous dragons in the broad-band manner come from excavations at Hsin Cheng in Honan, from tombs which range in date from about 900 B.C. to the late seventh or early sixth centuries. These were not systematically recorded, but the excavations at the cemetery of the Kuo state in Honan (p. 135 above) produced several intact grave-groups of bronze vessels similar in shapes and ornament to the earlier part of the Hsin Cheng find. Since the age of the Kuo tombs is deemed not to descend below 655 B.C. we are on good ground in attributing the broad-band style of dragons to the two centuries between 900 and 700 B.C.

The bronzes of the Hsin Cheng and Kuo graves cover the period when the Chou rulers were experiencing great pressure from the barbarians inhabiting the north-western region enclosed in the great loop of the Yellow river. Attacks by the Jung compelled the king to move his seat to Loyang in 771 B.C. (See p. 113.) Between 660 and 640 the Ti held the territory of Wei in north Honan. With the Jung they attacked Loyang in 648 and then proceeded to operate against the state of Cheng lying south of the Yellow river. King Hsiang, who had married a Ti princess, was driven from his royal domain in 636. Sporadic inroads of nomads continued into the sixth century. One archaeological trace of this infiltration is probably the spread of crouched burials along the Yellow river valley (*see* p. 128 above). The degree of contact between the settled

Fig. 46 Harness cheek-piece of bronze. 8th-7th century B.C. British Museum. Scale 1:2

Figs. 47-49

Fig. 47 Interlaced
dragons from a
bronze vessel found
at Hsin Cheng,
Honan. 8th - early
7th century B.C.

Chinese and nomadic peoples in the north-west we may suppose to have been much closer than is implied in the histories'
contrast between Chinese and 'barbarians'. Ethnically the two
groups were akin and the economic aspects of life which
separated them were not immutable for either.

In the light of these events it is not surprising, even as early
as the eighth or seventh centuries B.C., to find trends in Chinese
art which two or three centuries later can be identified in the
art of the nomads of the Asiatic steppes, on their harness
bronzes and decorated knives. The nomads had a strong taste
for pure geometric pattern, spirals, beading, rope-twists and
plaits, which they combined with their fantastic animal themes.
Some of these minor geometric motifs appear on the Hsin
Cheng vessels.

Fig. 47

INTER-
LACERY
AND LOCAL
NORTHERN
STYLES

A great feature of steppe art as we know it later is interlacery. Pattern of this kind was probably inspired by the plaiting
of ropes and thongs with which as horsemen and breeders of
horses they were so much concerned. The Shang and early
Chou patterns seem almost deliberately to avoid inter-
weaving the lines of their figures, however complicated. But at

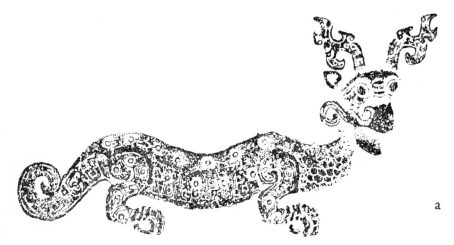

a

Hsin Cheng interlacery appears, at first timidly, applied to ribbon-like dragons whose ancestry is to be sought on vessels of the ninth century. The date of these dragons at Hsin Cheng is perhaps a hundred years later. The band of interlacery is often decorated in engraved line with a repeated figure: a brief spiral curling on to the base of an elongated triangle—the 'volute and triangle' of the art historians. The dragon has become merely a long line, usually doubled, terminating in a head which gets increasingly bird-like. Interlaced pattern appears also in tight, squared units. In the transformation of the dragon heads we may see an influence from, or perhaps the origin of, the griffin head which figures so prominently in steppe art. Last to appear are units of pattern consisting of tight-packed curved and hooked elements with a scatter of eyes, unintelligible except as a degeneration of interlaced pattern from which the crossings are omitted. This occurs on a series of tall vases which resemble so closely pieces we shall presently describe from a tomb 600 miles away to the south-west, at Shou Hsien in Anhui province, that one might think them products of the same workshop.

Fig. 48a, b

Fig. 49

Fig. 48 a, b, Dragon motifs used in the decoration of bronze vessels found at Hsin Cheng Honan. 7th Century B.C. (from rubbings)

b

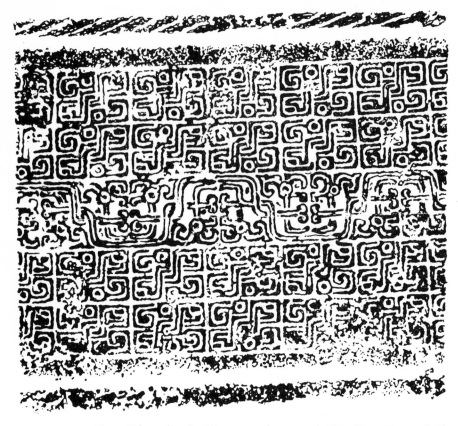

Fig. 49 Diaper of interlaced dragons on a bronze vessel. Hsin Cheng, Honan. 7th-6th century B.C.

The smaller repetitive units of design found on the latest-looking groups of bronze vessels from Hsin Cheng clearly were impressed on to the casting moulds with a stamp. As far as we can tell this method was never resorted to in the Shang and early Chou periods, when in the best works the bronze ornament has a vitality inseparable from the individual wax model necessary for each piece. The use of the stamp and the covering of surfaces with the small identical motifs which it encouraged set a fashion in decorative art which was to per‑ sist until the end of the Chou period. On the Hsin Cheng vessels decorated on their main surfaces by this means—and as if to compensate for the monotony of it—animals modelled fully in the round were added as handles, bases or finials. Tall vases stand on a pair of tigers, and tigers with reverted heads cling to the sides. Tortuous dragon‑handles reflect the same baroque tendency. On these animals curled snouts, heart‑ shaped ears, feet formed of double rounded claws and the peculiar circle and brief spiral set over the main limb joints are conventions which recur in steppe art, whether of southern Siberia or of the Ordos region of China.[5] They are common in Chinese art of the middle Chou period, from the late seventh to the fifth centuries, and their special connexion with bronze harness trappings is another pointer to the north‑west, the region of horse‑raising and of fraternisation of Chinese and nomad.

Plate 41

Fig. 48a

Plates 44,45

Plate 42

Plate 43

Before tracing the history of the late Hsin Cheng style, which takes us south of the Yellow river into the territory of the tur‑ bulent Ch'u state, we may glance at two local variants of the animal‑interlacery style in the north. One of these is named after the village of Li Yü in the north‑east corner of Shansi province, where an important find of bronze vessels was made in 1923. Here the spherical and oval vessels with conforming deep lids and ring‑base, or three small feet ('*ting*') are covered with engraved friezes of apparently continuous interlacery of dragons, which on closer inspection proves to be a repetition of identical stamped units. The ribbon of the interlacery is filled with close spirals and near‑triangles not much different from those we noted in Hsin Cheng. Volutes are placed at the end of a ribbon, or at points where it turns in a right angle. This ornament often includes a stylised full‑face animal mask based on a ram's‑head, and the lids are decorated with

Plate 40

naturalistic sheep, buffalo or birds, three of each on a vessel, sensitively modelled in the round. Monster masks surmount the stumpy legs. The masks suggest a revival of the *t'ao t'ieh*, but the resemblance is remote. There is no longer the hint of magic. The vessels may have been used in sacrifice, but they have now acquired a secular elegance, suited to more festive and mundane occasions. The panels of decoration are often separated by a relief pattern of plaited rope. The Li Yü bronzes belong probably to the late seventh or the sixth centuries B.C. They are some of the most attractive products of Chou art.

Figs. 50, 51   Ornament related to that of Li Yü is seen on bronzes ex, cavated in 1953 at Chia Ko Chuang near T'ang Shan in Hopei province. One of these is a *tui*, a nearly globular vessel which appears for the first time about 500 B.C., and another a *yi*, a water container, made here to a notably individual design.[6] But one elegant vase introduces a style of decoration unknown at Li Yü or Hsin Cheng. It consists of animated hunting

Figs. 52, 53   scenes, figures of men and animals crisply drawn in panels formed by the plaited rope carrying-cradle which is simulated

Fig. 50 Bronze hu. *From Chao Ku near, Hui Hsien, Honan. Height 37·8 cm.*

166

in bronze on the sides of the vase. The animals include boar, deer and birds, which would appear to be real game. A fanciful phoenix-like bird is among them and a creature resembling an elephant, which is no less imaginary in this setting, since elephant have not lived wild in Central China in historical times. The huntsmen are armed with spears and one is followed by a dog. A number of similar 'hunting *hu*' are preserved in collections, but hitherto no find-place had been recorded. One shows bowmen shooting at birds with arrows to which cords are attached (intended probably to help in recovering them), and a chariot driven by a man wearing an animal mask, as if a kind of sympathetic magic were part of a hunting ritual. Another famous piece includes a hunting scene with others illustrating a great variety of activities. Another hunting hu, the only inscribed piece which is known, commemorates a sacrifice at a place in the territory of Yen, in the modern province of Hopei. The Yen state maintained its independence from the eighth century B.C. until it was overthrown by Ch'in shortly before the unification of 232 B.C. Its territory included the modern Hopei and extended far to the north-east.

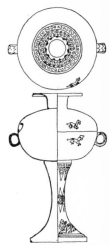

Fig. 51 Bronze tou, from Chia Ko Chuang, T'ang Shan. Height 35.5 cm.

We can readily imagine that in the sixth century B.C. the population of this region stood to tribes inhabiting Manchuria and the forested tracts beyond the Amur river in much the same relation as the Chinese of the north-west did to the Jung and Ti. Here as in the north-west cultural influences emanating from the barbarians could be transmitted to the Central Plain. Some such connexion may account for the appearance of the 'hunting style' in the state of Yen. In China the style is anomalous: the pictures it presents of the hunt in progress are curiously reminiscent of the rock drawings of primitive huntsmen, whether in Africa or at the opposite end of Asia in the Karelian isthmus. Some figures of tigers and dragons represented in line on flat surfaces at Chia Ko Chuang recall the flamboyant plastic animals of Hsin Cheng vases, but the scales and dots

Fig. 54

which fill the outlines are distinctive. They are the Hopei variant of an animal style which was now due to spread from the Central Plain into the Yangtse valley.

BRONZES OF THE CH'U STATE

By 500 B.C. the lower-lying region south of the Huai Yang mountains, forming the middle basin of the Yangtze river with its system of lakes and tributaries, was under the control of the powerful Ch'u state, whose rapid expansion and aggression against its northern neighbours was now a dominant factor in the politics of the feudal states. A large number of bronze vessels, weapons and ornaments that have reached collections during the past thirty years came from tombs in the vicinity of Shou Hsien, a city of the state of Wu, which was annexed by Ch'u in 473 B.C. This sudden appearance of fine bronze-craft in an area in which no metallurgy seems to have been practised in the earlier Chou period is a sign of the wealth and sinicisation of a people whom the northerners had looked on as barbarians. The Ch'u art appears in bronze fully fledged. Much of it so closely resembles the style of the later group of vessels found at Hsin Cheng that one might think the new southern style to be derived from it. But the very abundance of the finds at Shou Hsien suggests that there was here an inventive bronze centre, which produced its own version of the ornament and animal motifs now fashionable farther north, possibly influenced by a local artistic tradition which had not

Fig. 55

Fig. 52 Decoration of a bronze vase ('hunting hu') *in the Kunstindustri-Museum, Copenhagen. 5th Century B.C. Scale approx. 1:3*

Fig. 53 Decoration on a bronze hu. 5th-4th century B.C. The scenes include target practice with the bow and the picking of mulberry leaves (top register); shooting birds, pounding rice (?) and playing music on bronze bells and musical stones (middle register); a battle on land and water (lowest register); National Museum, Peking. Scale. approx. 1:3

previously been expressed in metal. We may assume that by these times a trade in finished bronzes passed from state to state, ideas travelling rapidly from one workshop to another.

The motifs found on the bronzes from Shou Hsien were taken by Karlgren to define a Huai style, so called after the river on which the town stands. The style reveals the same partial

Plates 54, 55   kinship with the animal art of the Steppes as is seen in the two northern styles we have just discussed. Rope and plait patterns, spirals, scales, dots and hachuring commonly frame or fill the interlacery or the animals' bodies. A recurrent ground pattern is built of small units consisting of a brief spiral and an adjoin‐ing band bent in a hook, or resembling a feathered wing. The taste for bold plastic effects is more marked. Tigers and dragons are mounted on the sides of bronze vessels. Increasingly tight, squared interlacery of small scale fills panels of the décor.

Plates 42, 53   Dragon designs, in openwork, in which the form of the animal is all but lost in a flurry of small spirals, and comma‐shaped

Fig. 54 Dragon and tiger depicted on a bronze dish (p'an). *From Chia Ko Chuang, near T'ang Shan, Hopei. Scale approx 1:1*

Fig. 55 Bronze vessels and bells from the tomb of the Marquis of Ts'ai at Shou Hsien, Anhui. Early 5th century B.C. Scale 1:21

a

Fig. 56 Bronze openwork ornament, probably for harness. From Chung Chou Lu, Loyang near Honan. 5th century B.C. Scale 3:4

figures furnish the magnificent handles of bells which now seem to be indispensable in the bronze treasury of a great house.

To our eyes the trend of Chinese bronze art is now towards decorative effect at the expense of more arresting architectonic and symbolic designs of the earlier period. The force of the mythology which had dictated the mysterious ancient themes is spent, the pleasure of the eye is now the only aim. That part which Huai art shares with Steppe art, the distortion of animals' bodies and their combination with subordinate geometric figures, has lost some of the dynamic quality which in the art of the steppe nomads hints at the sympathy of the primitive hunts-man with the muscle and spirit, even the supernatural life of his prey. This more condescending approach to the animal world taken by the artists of civilised China is analogous to the development of the steppe art at the far western end of its vast extension. Here contact with the Greek colonies on the Black

Fig. 58 Decoration of a lacquered box. From Yang Tzŭ Shan, near Chengtu, Szechwan. 4th century B.C.

b

Sea coast produced a hybrid art in which traditional Steppe motifs were softened by the imitation of classical naturalism. In both regions animals were depicted in a gentler mood, with a comfortable condescension. In China of the sixth and fifth centuries B.C. this naturalism is seen at its best in the small animals—goats, birds and oxen—set on the lids of some of the bronze vessels.

By the beginning of the fourth century B.C. the Huai style seems to have ousted the lingering styles of Middle Chou everywhere. We observe its further development taking a banal turn. The purely geometric elements came to dominate, first the spiral and triangle motif, and then a squared geometric figure representing a delicate abstraction of the interlaced bands.

Fig. 57 a, b, Bronze belt-hooks. 4th-3rd century B.C. British Museum. Scale 2:5

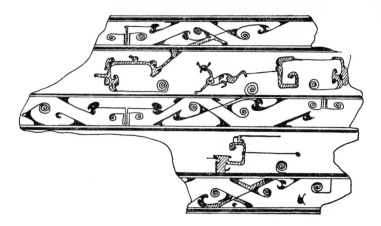

Fig. 59 Decoration of a lacquered toilet box (lien). From Ch'ang Sha, Hunan. 3rd century B.C.

Fig. 60

Plates 58, 59, 62, 69, 70

Figs. 62, 63

Fig. 60 Silver-inlaid design in bronze shaft-pole mount. From Yang Tzŭ Shan near Chengtu. Szech-wan. c. 300 B.C.

informed with a cold, draughtsman-like vigour of ruler and compass. The units of design are repeated over the whole surface of the bronzes, contrasting thin and broad lines and enriched with gold, silver or turquoise inlay, more rarely embellished with roundels of the newest material, glass. This geometricising trend is found in central China, where it is exemplified in the bronzes from the rich shaft-tomb at Chin Ts'un in Honan, excavated clandestinely in 1936, and more recently at Hsin Yang in the same province and in the numer-ous tombs around Ch'ang Sha in Hunan. The geometric motifs are designed with increasing attention to symmetry about a vertical axis in each unit of the pattern, or are set in corres-ponding pairs in heraldic fashion.

At Ch'ang Sha these motifs are used on some cups, toilet-boxes, shields and sword scabbards made of lacquer. This is the juice of the tree *Rhus vernicifera*, which applied in thin, successively dried layers to a base of wood or cloth provides a hard, durable surface which can be polished to a high lustre and painted. The abundance in the Ch'ang Sha tombs of *Fig. 59* lacquered objects painted in red and yellow on a black ground suggests that the craft was practised near-by. The lacquer tree may have grown in central China in those times, although today it is not known much beyond the confines of Szechwan province.

The Ch'ang Sha workshops continued active well into Han times, when their products and those of their imitators were spread through the empire. The lacquer industry was officially patronised. Lacquer cups and boxes were an important commodity in the gifts made to Hunnish chieftains

Fig. 61 Pottery with painted decoration. From Shao Kou, near Loyang, Honan. 4th century B.C. Scale approx. 1:10

Fig. 62 Design on the lid of a bronze tou. From Ch'ang Sha. 3rd century B.C. Scale approx. 2:3

beyond the north-west frontiers, and together with the tribute occasionally offered in return provided a kind of foreign trade. Such articles seem also to have been a perquisite of high government officials, especially, to judge from their frequency in tombs of the Chinese colony of Lolang in Korea, of officials who accepted appointments far from home. Conforming to the views of economists who advocated state monopoly as a means of preventing the dangerous growth of mercantile wealth in private hands, Han government assumed the control of the lacquer factories. The evidence for its organisation comes from the first century B.C. It is reasonable to suppose, however, that the Han workshops continued methods established earlier by the makers of the Ch'ang Sha lacquers of the third century. The minuteness of the division of labour and the careful supervision no doubt continued traditions of craftsmanship as practised under princely patronage in feudal times.[7]

An inscription on a wine-cup dated to A.D. 4 illustrates the working of a lacquer factory, in this case the West Factory, one of five recorded from Han times. All of these factories were in

Szechwan, the region favoured by *Rhus vernicifera.* The italicised words are personal names:

'4th year of Yüan Shih [A.D. 4]. Shu [Szechwan] com-mandery, West Factory. Imperial cup of wood, lacquered, engraved and painted, with gilded handles. Capacity one shéng, 16 yüeh. Initial work, *Yi.* Application of lacquer, *Li.* Top work, *Tang.* Gilding of bronze handles, *Ku.* Painting, *Ting.* Engraving, *Fêng.* Finishing, *P'ing.* Pro-duction, *Tsung Tsao.* Official in charge of the soldiers of the factory guard, *Chang.* Manager, *Liang.* Deputy, *Fêng.* Assist-ant, *Lung.* Head clerk, *Pao Chu.*'

One notes from the inscriptions that workmen seldom held a post for more than two or three years before they were re-placed, seldom to reappear. The senior officials enjoyed on average only a slightly longer tenure of office. The favour of office, it seems, was of short duration in the Han bureaucracy.

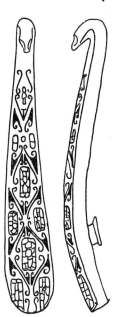

Fig. 63 Bronze belt-hook with inlay of silver and turquoise. From Chung Chou Lu, near Loyang, Honan. About 300 B.C. Scale 2:3

It is less surprising that officialdom was conservative in its taste. Until the latter half of the first century A.D. the official workshops repeated with little change, and that for the worse, designs derived in the late third and early second centuries B.C. from the bronze décor of the latest Chou style; although, to judge from the decoration of other contemporary objects in bronze and clay, these designs were already old-fashioned.

Some wooden effigies found in tombs at Ch'ang Sha con-trast strangely with the sophisticated elegance of the bronzes and lacquers that lay with them. Many of them are roughly shaped human figures, placed in the grave to serve the dead in the next world. Others are figures of beings connected appa-rently with the after-life of the dead, for similar figures are painted on silk together with a text (not yet fully deciphered) dealing with like matter. One carving represents two cranes standing on a pedestal formed of two entwined snakes. The bodies of birds and snakes alike are decorated with designs in black, red and yellow lacquer paint; where the pattern is not conventional scales and feathers, it repeats the volute-and-triangle unit with internal spirals derived from the late feudal bronze style, which is foreign to Han art outside the archaising lacquer cups and boxes. Other figures display goggle-eyed heads with protruding fangs and pendant tongue, or, like the piece now in the British Museum, a human head with long protruding tongue and carrying deer's antlers. It was thought at first that this 'un-Chinese' sculpture and the chthonic cult connected with it were lingering remnants of the unsinicised culture of the southern barbarians, but recently the discovery of similar highly coloured, grotesque wooden carvings at Hsin Yang in south Honan carried the evidence of the superstition and its queer imagery into the ancient centre of Chinese civilisation.[8]

The blocking-out style of carving used on some of these images is reminiscent of the style of some of the effigies carved

Plate 75

Plate 76

Plate 71

Plate 72

Fig. 64

Fig. 64 Figures decorating a lacquered musical instrument. 4th-3rd century B.C. From Hsin Yang, Honan

in the Moï jungle of western Indo-China for the corner-posts of tomb-houses. The antlers on the British Museum head recall the antlered god or deified reindeer which figures in animistic and totemistic cult and legend spread from northern Europe across northern Asia to Siberia. In recent times the antlers on the head of a shaman in southern Siberia were described as a symbol of his capacity for rapid motion. The shaman, and his Chinese equivalent, the *wu*, was ever closely concerned with funeral rites; one of his tasks—though this does not seem to have been explicitly recorded in China—was to conduct the souls of the dead to their last resting-place. He used his magical powers, often achieved in an ecstatic trance, to traverse space and to pass between the worlds of men, gods and ghosts. The importance of the crane in Taoist fable is enough to connect it with the circle of shamanistic lore. Indeed the heavenly gods, feathered men and mystic animals of the Taoist mythology as it appears in Han times no doubt came from the same body of beliefs as lay behind the wooden effigies of Ch'ang Sha and Hsin Yang. Through the interest which Han emperors took in Taoist magic, these superstitions became more respectable as artistic themes.

Apart from the cult-figures there is nothing found in the Ch'ang Sha tombs, either weapon forms or artistic motifs, which departs radically from the main stream of Chinese tradition. In areas to the south-west and south, however, regions beyond the pale of Chinese civilisation, local bronze cultures flourishing in the last few centuries B.C. bore an individual stamp in art and artifacts. These cultures developed in comparative isolation and their remains reflect local differences. The Dong-son culture of northern Indo-China owes nothing to Chou China, unless it be the bare technique of casting in bronze, and that remains doubtful. In Szechwan, Yunnan and south Kuantung (the region around Hong Kong), Chinese weapons, swords, ko-halberds and spearheads were adopted, but with some original modifications, and the decoration applied to the bronze was of local growth. In boat-shaped wooden coffins in Szechwan, alongside ko and swords of Chou type and ring-handled knives of the Han type, were found many examples of short swords with a simple tang instead of the usual cast hilt. The blades of these are decorated with curious motifs, of which the commonest are a hand and serpent-figure and a tiger accompanied by shapes possibly representing a trap. In Szechwan and Yunnan are found bronze socketed axes of rectangular section and expanded blades, distinct from those of central China; and from Yunnan comes one example of a ko on which a socket is cast,

Fig. 37

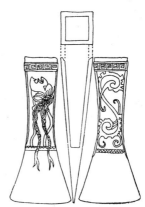

Fig. 65 Decorated socketed axe of bronze.
From Shih Chai Shan. 1st century B.C.
Scale approx. 1:4

although it retains the part which in the normal type passes through the wooden haft and projects above it. More striking, however, than these modifications of standard weapon and tool forms is the originality of the artistic ideas interpreted in bronze.

The richest collection of bronzes found thus far in the southern territories was contained in a tomb at Shih Chai Shan, near Kunming in Yunnan province. History relates events which suggest how Chinese influence, and with it possibly the earliest knowledge of bronze working, first penetrated to this region. In 334 B.C. King Ch'ing Hsiang of Ch'u sent an expedition to the Tien lake on whose east shore the hill of Shih Chai Shan is situated, and the expeditionaries lingered there until their homeward route was cut off by the forces of the Ch'in at the moment of this state's dramatic expansion. Their general is reported to have remained permanently at his out-post and to have founded a state and a kingship. The Shih Chai Shan tomb is dated to about 100 B.C. by mirrors and vessels of Han type, evidently imported, which it contained. The place had been inhabited much longer, from a time when cropping was combined with the gathering of fresh-water

Figs. 65, 66

Fig. 66

Plate 73

Plate 74

molluscs. A smaller grave near-by contained a body laid on its side with flexed legs, accompanied by a few rough pots, recalling the similar burials found in Kansu, Shensi and Honan.

Some fragments of bronze drums excavated at Shih Chai Shan have ornament of birds, and human figures in huge plumed hats rowing in a boat, quite similar to that of the famous drums from Dong-son. Some of the minor motifs, small circles, groups of parallel lines in bands and loops, hachuring, etc., can be compared to similar 'filling' devices in Huai art, but the resemblance is a cousinship rather than a direct borrowing. The original part of this Yunnan bronze art, an astonishing skill in naturalistic modelling in the round, is unique and excels anything of the kind known either from China or south-east Asia. The figures of animals, bulls, tigers, birds, placed on the sockets of axes or cast as separate ornaments, are designed wholly in the round, with a pictorial realism un-paralleled in the more conventionalised and graphic designs of the Chinese and the northern nomads. Whereas so little of the bronze art we have described hitherto is concerned with depicting real activities, the Yunnan artists represent scenes of fighting animals, huntsmen and their prey, village festivities and ceremonial which they must have seen with their own eyes. Tigers and wolf-like creatures are shown attacking cattle and deer, a group of huntsmen pin down a tiger under their spears, mounted hunters and warriors with armour and helmets are shown at the gallop, or leaping at a tiger or boar. Musicians and dancers in elaborate costume stand in rows or gesticulate with outspread arms and legs. Still more of social life is re-vealed by scenes of fully modelled figures placed on the top of bronze stands (termed 'cowrie-shell holders' by the excavators), which copy the shape of the bronze drums. In one scene a high-gabled hut shelters rows of drummers squatting beside their instruments, surrounded by a crowd of villagers who seem

Fig. 66 Decoration on the sides of a bronze drum. From Shih Chai Shan. 1st century B.C. Scale approx. 1:4

to be talking together excitedly. The scene where a bull is issuing from a low door in a wall on which rows of spectators are seated suggests a festival of bull-catching such as may still be seen performed in southern India. Other crowded groups represent elaborate religious ceremonial. In one a woman, perhaps a priestess or chieftainess, sits on a throne at the centre, surrounded by thirteen further women and three men, some of whom hold up offerings to her while others appear to be en-gaged in plaiting and other unidentifiable tasks. The double-coiled buns of the women are like those still worn by the Miao women of south-west China at the present time. In another scene of some fifty individuals a pillar standing at the centre is entwined with a serpent and supports a tiger. An execution or human sacrifice seems to be in progress, the victim tied down on a board. A priestess sits on a high throne. Some of the figures carry firewood and baskets of fish. In these compositions the modelling of the figures is crude, but fresh and expressive. Some processions of people with animals and carrying female notables in sedan-chairs are engraved on the flat surfaces of drums. They are depicted with the same free realism, and the same imagination and skill is displayed in relating them con-vincingly to each other.

In pursuing the spread of Chinese influence into the 'un-opened' territory beyond the area of metropolitan Chinese culture, we have described from Yunnan a phenomenon which repeats the history of the north and centre of China. As soon as it was known, bronze was used not only to produce weapons, no doubt the initial incentive behind the mastery of bronze-casting, but to produce ritual and artistic objects besides. The weapons varied only a little from the Chinese forms they copied, but the bronze art perpetuated a local tradition of plastic and linear subjects. The drums apart (which may have been imports from northern Indo-China) this art is independent equally of the art of south-east Asia exemplified by the Dong-son finds, and of the art of Ch'u and central China. The compositions of fighting animals and horsemen have affinities with the art of the nomads living far to the north, but its plain plastic freedom is distinctive and original. Apart from this resemblance of artistic themes, which is never very close there is no evidence yet of historical connexion between Yunnan and north-west China or the steppes of southern Siberia.

SCULPTURE
AND JADE
CARVING

No monumental sculpture and very little free modelling in the round, even on a small scale, is found in the Shang and Chou periods. The absence of a tradition of stone building is perhaps enough to account for the lack of the former. Probably in earlier as in later times the wooden buildings of the Chinese gave no place for large-scale carving, and they did not nurture the mason's craft which underlies a tradition of stone-carving.

Fig. 67

Plate 16

Plates 37, 60

The conventionalised figures of birds and animals carved in limestone which were placed in the great Shang tombs ceased to be made with the fall of the dynasty. The rare bronze figures of human beings made in the Chou period are small, seldom exceeding a height of four or five inches, and for the most part lack the vitality of the animal themes. The human form was evidently less keenly studied than were animal subjects. One might speak of an aversion from depicting men.

Figs. 23, 43, 68

Jade-carving during the Shang and earlier Chou period was confined to flat forms of animals serving as amulets and dress

Fig. 67 Limestone owl. From Hsi Pei Kang, near Anyang, Honan. Shang period. Scale approx. 1:3

ornaments, and the ritual objects: the perforated disc called *pi*, the pillar-shaped *tsung* (explained respectively in later tradition as symbols of heaven and earth), the *huang* crescent, and cere-monial knives and halberd blades. The expansion of jade-carving which took place from the fifth century B.C. adapts the decorative schemes of the bronze décor, the animal shapes and the small-scale repetitive ornament echoing motifs which may be seen in greater elaboration on bronze. Jade was in-creasingly used for personal adornment. The sword-guards, scabbard mounts and ornaments of the dress and person made of it have a perfection of design and execution which was never to be surpassed in the long subsequent history of jade-carving in China.

Plates 63, 64, 65, 66, 67

The end of the Chou period closes a great cycle in the history of Chinese art. It embraces more than a millennium of singularly logical development. At the advent of Han art, with its wider horizons in which human activities, landscape, vegetation and architectural forms were encompassed, and still more with the arrival in the early centuries of the Christian era of western influences of which the Buddhist religion proved the most lasting, we have quitted the world of Bronze Age China and stand at the beginning of artistic traditions which have lasted to modern times. But the inventions of the ancients never lost their appeal. Particularly in the decorative art of the Sung and later dynasties the shapes of ritual bronze vessels and of ritual jades, dragons and *t'ao t'ieh* appear again as solemn evocations of the past.

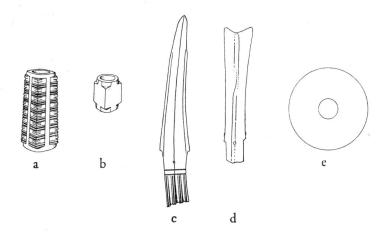

Fig. 68 Ritual jades of the Shang period. a, b, tsung: *c, d, knives; e,* pi. *British Museum. Scale 1:10*

1 J. G. Anderson discovered the deposits in 1921. On the evidence of teeth, Davidson Black named the new type of man in 1927. The first skull was found by Pei Wen-chung two years later. To date, parts of the skeletons of over forty-five individuals have been recovered. The first found and best preserved of the skulls was lost when the Japanese occupied Peking in 1941. In 1959 excavations were resumed.

2 The principal argument for an earlier neolithic stage, ante-dating the Yang Shao culture, is based on material from a few sites in Shensi. But the Sha Yuan culture of central Shensi belongs to the Gobi tradition, and has no better claim than the Gobi sites to be regarded as a neolithic precursor of the Yang Shao, although the presence of polished stone shows neolithic influence. At Tou Chi T'ai, near Pao Chi, farther west in central Shensi, the pottery is however more primitive, and although distinct from that of Yang Shao (painted pottery being absent), may, like the pottery found on Gobi sites, be no earlier in date.

3 Andersson makes the Ch'i Chia P'ing culture of Kansu the earliest of his succession of cultures. It has plain black pottery with angular profiles, and is quite distinct from the painted wares. The writer accepts Hsia Nai's argument for a later date for it. *cf.* *K'ao Ku Hsüeh Pao*, vol. III, pp. 101-117.

4 *K'ao Ku Hsüeh Pao*, 1955, No. 10, pp. 27 ff.

CHAPTER II

1 Hsiao T'un is a village 3 km. north-west of the modern prefectural town of Anyang. The latter name is often used to denote the Shang site.

2 In archaeological literature the dynasty is called by either name, and sometimes 'Shang-Yin'.

3 Dates argued from historical sources for the defeat of the Shang by the Chou vary from 1027 B.C., which is the latest to 1122

B.C., which is the earliest and that given by the orthodox traditional chronology. In recent times dates derived from the historical text called the Bamboo Books have gained increasing credence. From the current version of this text C. Bishop derives his dates of 1558 and 1050 for the beginning and end of Shang rule. Wang Kuo-wei deduced from his reconstitution of what he considered to be the authentic text the dates 1523 and 1027, and these figures have been accepted by Ch'en Meng-chia in his recent studies. According to the Bamboo Books 273 years intervened between the accession of P'an Keng, who moved his capital to Hsiao T'un, and the defeat of the last Shang king. This gives the year 1300 B.C. for the establishment of P'an Keng's capital. Other texts can be found to strengthen the argument for 1523 as the beginning of the Shang reign, as against the 1765 of the orthodox list.

4   As suggested by Mizuno Seiichi in *An Outline of World Archeology* (*Sekai Kōkogaku Taikei*), Eastern Asia II, p. 9.

5   The circumstances in which Academia Sinica carried out its fifteen campaigns of excavation at Anyang before the recent war were far from ideal. The occasional approach of bandits and the hostility of local villagers long accustomed to profit from their own treasure-hunts added to the difficulty of the work. The chances of establishing stratigraphy were reduced through the disturbance caused by the illicit digging. The villagers had located tombs by a probing method of their own invention. The outbreak of the war with Japan interrupted the official excavations, which ceased in the spring of 1937 and could not be resumed before 1950. The pre-war excavated material had by then been removed to Formosa, where some of it still awaits detailed publication.

6   The rammed-earth wall at the Lung Shan site of Ch'eng Tzǔ Yai in Shantung province, hitherto much invoked as further evidence of the close connexion of the Shang and Lung Shan cultures, is now thought possibly to belong to the late Chou period.

7   Unfortunately no complete report of the excavations has been published. Summaries have appeared by Li Chi and Shih Chang-ju (see bibliography), who were among those in charge of the pre-war excavations, and others more recently printed on the mainland by Ch'en Meng-chia and Hu Hou-hsüan. The main finds are, how-

ever, by now well known in illustration. For the trace of the plans of the eight great tombs we rely on a brief survey (*cf.* Li Chi, 'On the development of the white pottery at Yin Hsü', Bulletin of the Institute of History and Philology, Academia Sinica, xxviii (1925) p. 861).

8　There is no evidence for the double-curved bow in Japan. Here, from the eighth century A.D. onwards at least, the bow, of compound structure, is shaped in a single arc, but balanced for holding and nocking the arrow nearer one end by about a quarter of the length. This device made it more suitable for shooting from the saddle, in spite of its considerable length.

9　Loehr M., *Chinese Bronze Age Weapons*, pp. 100-4.

10　The nomenclature of the bronze vessels is a study apart. The terms used in this book are those accepted today, and for the most part were adopted by the Sung antiquarians. The modern pronunciations differ from the ancient readings. The correspondence of character to vessel is far from certain in many cases, particularly for the Shang and early Chou shapes. *Ting, li, kuei, ku, chüeh* are among those which are most reliably identified. In later Chou times the use of vessel names was not consistent (differences of dialect contributing to this). A generic name *yi*, i.e. a sacrificial vessel, was often used by the Shang for a variety of forms. Yetts deals abundantly with the nomenclature in his writings.

11　The texts and published source for the oracle sentences quoted here will be found in Ch'en Meng-chia's *Comprehensive Account of the Oracle Texts from Yin Hsü*.

12　Of the eight kings whom Wang Kuo-wei failed to identify Tung Tso-pin points out that the last two were unlikely to be named as ancestral spirits, and he found equivalents for the remainder, completing the total of thirty. Of these identifications Kuo Mo-jo doubts two, the names of the fifth and fifteenth kings.

13　*cf.* Kaizuka Shigeki's study of a group of bronzes found at Liang Shan, near Shou Chang Hsien, Shantung province, in his *Development of the Historical Study of Ancient China (Chūgoku Kodai Shigaku Hatten*), pp. 369 ff.

14　*cf.* Kaizuka Shigeki, *op. cit.*, p. 267.

15　Quoted by Kaizuka Shigeki, *op. cit.*, pp. 264, 116.

China

CHAPTER III

   1 *cf.* Kaizuka Shigeki, *Development of the Historical Study of Ancient China* (*Chūgoku Kodai Shigaku Hatten*), p. 309.

   2 The famous Sung Ting of the reign of King K'ung, late tenth century B.C. This inscription is translated in W. Willetts, *Chinese Art*, p. 125.

   3 This inscription is translated in full by P. Yetts in the Catalogue of the Eumorfopoulos Collection, Vol. I, p. 27–29.

   4 Wen Wu Ts'an K'ao Tzu Liao, 1955, No. 5, pp. 58 ff. Watson, W. *Archaeology in China*, pp. 23–24.

   5 i.e. of the type seen on Plate XXXV, No. 87, in M. Loehr's *Chinese Bronze Age Weapons*, No. 88 on the same plate belongs to a group of swords which Loehr places in general before the swords with cast hilt, but excavations published after the appearance of his book (*cf. Archaeological Journal* [*Kao Ku Hsüeh Pao*] 1958, No. 2, pp. 77 ff.) show that they are much later, probably of the fourth century B.C., and a barbarian product of the south-west.

   6 Kuo Yü. Quoted and translated in J. Needham, *The Development of Iron and Steel Technology in China*, p. 2.

   7 *K'ao Ku Hsüeh Pao*, 1957, No. 3, pp. 93 ff.

   8 Ku T'ieh-fu. Some archaeological questions concerning grave 52.826 at Ch'ang Sha, in Wen Wu, 1954, No. 10.

   9 Li Cheng-kuang, 'Iron objects of the Warring States period found at Ch'ang Sha and Heng Yang', *K'ao Ku T'ung Hsün*, 1956, No. 1.

  10 Sekino Takeshi, *Studies in Chinese Archaeology* (*Chūgoku Kōkogaku Kenyū*), *An examination of the early Iron Age of China*, pp. 162 ff.

CHAPTER IV

   1 Karlgren, B., *Catalogue of the Chinese Bronzes in the Alfred F. Pillsbury Collection*, Plates 20, 21.

   2 Hansford, S. H., *The Seligman Collection of Oriental Art*, Vol. I, Plate I.

   3 *cf.* Sun Tso-yün. On the theory that the T'ien Wang Kuei was made before Wu Wang's defeat of the Shang, *Wen Wu Ts'an K'ao Tzŭ Liao*, 1958, No. 1, pp. 29 ff.

   4 *cf.* White, W. C., *Bronze Culture of Ancient China*, pp. 118 ff. and Plate LXI, the 'Mang Shan Set'.

5   *cf.* bronzes of the Tagar culture of Minusinsk, of the seventh to
    second centuries B.C. S. V. Kiselev, *The Ancient History of Southern
    Siberia* (*Drevnaya Istoriya Yuzhnoi Sibiri*), Plates XX, XXI.

6   Watson, W., *Archaeology in China*, pp. 27–28.

7   Watson, W., Chinese lacquered wine-cups, *British Museum Quart-
    erly*, Vol. XXI (1957) p. 21. ff.

8   Watson, W., A grave-guardian from Ch'ang Sha, *British Museum
    Quarterly*, Vol. XVII (1952) pp. 52–56.

9   *Wen Wu*, 1958, No. 1.

Select Bibliography

BMFEAS Bulletin of the Museum of Far Eastern Antiquities, Stockholm.

KKHP K'ao Ku Hsüch Pao (Archaeological Reports).

Tr. OCS Transactions of the Oriental Ceramic Society.

JRAS Journal of the Royal Asiatic Society.

The titles of Chinese and Japanese books and articles are translated. The
original titles of books only are given in brackets.

General

HISTORY

H. G. CREEL, *The Birth of China. A Survey of the Formative Period of
Chinese Civilization*. London, 1936.

H. G. CREEL, *Studies in Early Chinese Culture*. London, 1938.

W. EBERHARD, *A History of China*. London, 1950.

O. FRANKE, *Geschichte des Chinesischen Reiches*. Vol. I. Berlin, 1930.

G. B. GESSEY, *China's Geographic Foundations. A Survey of the Land and
its People*. New York, 1934.

A. HERRMANN, *Atlas of China*. Cambridge, Massachusetts, 1935.

SHIGEKI KAIZUKA, *The Development of the Historical Study of Ancient
China*. Tokyo, 1946 (Japanese: Chūgoku Kodai Shigaku Hatten).

O. LATTIMORE, *Inner Frontiers of Asia*. New York, 1940.

H. MASPERO, *La Chine Antique*. Paris, 1927.

TORAJIRŌ NAITŌ, *Ancient History of China*. Tokyo, 1944 (Japanese:
Shina Kodai-shi).

J. NEEDHAM, *Science and Civilization in China*. Vols. I, II. Cambridge,
1945, 1956.

ARCHAEOLOGY

J. G. ANDERSSON, *Children of the Yellow Earth*. London, 1934.

CHENG TE-K'UN, *Archaeology in China*. Vol. I. *Prehistoric China*.
Cambridge, 1959–60. Vol. II. *Shang China* (in progress).

LI CHI, *The Beginnings of Chinese Civilization.* Seattle, 1957.

SEIICHI MIZUNA (ed.), *An Outline of World Archaeology.* Vol. 6, *Eastern Asia II, the Yin-Chou Period.* Tokyo, 1958 (Japanese: Sekai Kōkogaku Taikei).

TAKESHI SEKINO, *Studies in Chinese Archaeology.* Tokyo, 1956 (Japanese: Chūgoku Kōkogaku Kenkyū, with English summary).

W. WATSON, *Archaeology in China.* London, 1960.

WEAPONS

CHOU WEI, *Draft of a History of Chinese Weapons.* Peking, 1957 (Chinese: Chung Kuo Ping Ch'i Shih Kao).

YOSHITO HARADA and KAZUCHIKA KOMAI (ed.), *Chinese Antiquities.* Part I, *Arms and Armour.* Part II, *Vessels and Vehicles.* Academy of Oriental Culture, Tokyo, 1932, 1937 (Japanese: Shina Koki Zukō).

M. LOEHR, *Chinese Bronze Age Weapons.* Ann Arbor, 1956.

ARTS

L. ASHTON and B. GRAY, *Chinese Art.* London, 1935.

L. BACHHOFER, *A Short History of Chinese Art.* London, 1944.

B. GRAY, *Early Chinese Pottery and Porcelain.* London, 1953.

S. H. HANSFORD, *Chinese Jade Carving.* London, 1950.

W. HOCHSTADTER, 'Pottery and Stonewares of Shang, Chou and Han.' *BMFEAS,* 24, 1952.

SEIICHI MIZUNO, *Bronzes and Jades of Ancient China.* Tokyo, 1959 (Japanese: Inshū Seidōki to Gyōku, with English summary).

L. SICKMAN and L. SOPER. *The Art and Architecture of China.* London, 1956.

O. SIREN, *Kinas Konst under Tre Artusenden.* Vol. I. Stockholm, 1942.

M. SULLIVAN, *An Introduction to Chinese Art.* London, 1960.

W. WILLETTS, *Chinese Art.* London, 1958.

MYTHOLOGY AND RITUAL

E. BIOT (Trans.), *Le Tcheou-li, ou Rites des Tcheou.* 2 vols. Paris, 1851.

M. GRANET, *Danses et Legendes de la Chine Ancienne.* Paris, 1926.

M. GRANET, *La Civilisation Chinoise.* Paris, 1929 (English translation London, 1930).

N

M. GRANET, *Fêtes et chansons anciennes de la Chine.* Paris, 1919 (English translation London, 1932).

M. GRANET, *La Pensée Chinoise.* Paris, 1934.

M. GRANET, *La Religion des Chinois.* Paris, 2nd ed. 1951.

M. GRANET, *La Féodalité Chinoise.* Oslo, 1952.

C. HENTZE, *Mythes et Symboles Lunaires.* Antwerp, 1932.

C. HENTZE, *Objets rituels, croyances et Dieux de la Chine Antique et de l'Amerique.* Antwerp, 1936.

C. HENTZE, *Frühchinesische Bronzen und Kulturdarstellungen.* 2 vols. Antwerp, 1937.

B. KARLGREN, 'Some Fecundity Symbols in Ancient China.' *BMFEAS,* 1930.

B. KARLGREN, 'Legends and Cults in Ancient China.' *BMFEAS,* 18, 1946.

B. LAUFER, *Jade: A Study in Chinese Archaeology and Religion.* Chicago, 1912.

SABURO MORIMIKI, *Ancient Chinese Myths.* Kyoto, 1944 (Japanese: Shina Kodai Shinwa).

F. WATERBURY, *Early Chinese Symbols and Literature: Vestiges and Speculations.* New York, 1942.

CATALOGUES OF COLLECTIONS AND EXHIBITIONS

THE CHINESE EXHIBITION. *A Commemorative Catalogue of the International Exhibition of Chinese Art.* London, 1936.

H. S. HANSFORD, *The Seligman Collection.* Vol. I. London, 1957.

S. JENYNS, *Chinese Archaic Jades in the British Museum.* London, 1951.

O. KARLBECK, *Chinese and Korean Bronzes at Hallwyl House, Stockholm.* Stockholm, 1938.

B. KARLGREN, 'Bronzes in the Hellström Collection.' *BMFEAS,* 20, 1948.

B. KARLGREN, 'Some Bronzes in the Museum of Far Eastern Antiquities.' *BMFEAS* 21, 1949.

B. KARLGREN, *A Catalogue of the Chinese Bronzes in the Alfred F. Pillsbury Collection.* Minneapolis, 1952.

F. C. KELLEY and CH'EN MENG-CHIA, *Chinese Bronzes from the Buckingham Collection.* Chicago, 1946.

J. E. KIDDER, *Early Chinese Bronzes in the City Art Museum of St Louis.* St Louis, 1956.

A. LETH, *Catalogue of Selected Objects of Chinese Art in the Museum of Decorative Art, Copenhagen.* Copenhagen, 1959.

J. E. LODGE, A. G. WENLEY and J. A. POPE, *Chinese Bronzes Acquired during the Administration of John Ellerton Lodge.* Freer Gallery of Art. Washington, 1946.

A. SALMONY, *Carved Jade of Ancient China.* Berkeley, 1938.

A. SALMONY, *Archaic Jades from the Sonnenschein Collection.* Chicago, 1952.

UMEHARA SUEJI, *The Flower of Ancient Chinese Bronzes.* 7 vols. Osaka, 1933–35 (Japanese: Shina Kōdō Seika).

W. P. YETTS, *The George Eumorfopoulos Collection. Catalogue of the Chinese and Korean Bronzes, Sculpture, Jade, Jewelry and Miscellaneous Objects.* 3 vols. London, 1929–32.

W. P. YETTS, *The Cull Chinese Bronzes.* London, 1939.

Palaeolithic and Mesolithic

M. BOULE, H. BREUIL, E. LICENT, P. TEILHARD DE CHARDIN, 'Le Paléolithique de la Chine.' *Archives de l'Institut de Paléontologie Humaine*, Memoire 4, Paris, 1928.

D. BLACK, P. TEILHARD DE CHARDIN, C. YOUNG, W. C. PEI, 'Fossil Man in China.' *Geological Survey of China.* Memoirs, Series A, No 11, Peking, 1933.

CHIA LAN-PO, *Early Man in the Ordos Region.* Shanghai, 1951. 2nd ed. 1955 (Chinese: Ho T'ao Jen).

CHIA LAN-PO, *Upper Cave Man.* Shanghai, 1951 (Chinese: Shan Ting Tung Jen).

KUO MO-JO, YANG CHUNG-CHIEN, PEI WEN-CHUNG *et al., The Discovery and Study of Human Fossils in China.* Peking, 1955 (Chinese: Chung Kuo Jen Lei Hua Shih Ti Fa Hsien Yü Yen Chiu).

J. MARINGER, 'Contribution to the Prehistory of Mongolia.' *Reports of the Sven Hedin Expedition.* Stockholm, 1950.

PEI WEN-CHUNG, 'An attempted correlation of Quaternary Geology, Palaeontology and Prehistory in Europe and China.' *Occasional Paper No 2 of the Institute of Archaeology of London University.* London, 1939.

PEI WEN-CHUNG, *Studies in Chinese Prehistory.* Shanghai, 1948 (Chinese: Chung Kuo Shih Ch'ien Shih Ch'i Chih Yen Chiu).

EXCAVATIONS

AN CHIH-MIN and WU JU-TSO, 'Neolithic sites in the region of Sha-yüan, at Ta Li and Chao-i, Shensi Province.' *KKHP*, 3, 1957 (Chinese).

J. G. ANDERSSON, 'An Early Chinese Culture.' *Geological Survey of China*. Peking, 1923.

J. G. ANDERSSON, 'Preliminary Report on Archaeological Research in Kansu.' *Geological Survey of China*. Peking, 1925.

J. G. ANDERSSON, 'Researches into the prehistory of the Chinese.' *BFMEAS*, 15, 1943.

J. G. ANDERSSON, 'Prehistoric Sites in Honan.' *BFMEAS*, 19, 1947.

CHENG TE-K'UN, *Archaeological Studies in Szechwan*. Cambridge, 1957.

D. J. FINN, *Archaeological Finds on Lamma Island near Hong Kong*. Hong Kong, 1958.

FUKIEN PROVINCE CULTURAL PROPERTIES COMMISSION, 'Investigation of a Neolithic Site at Yun Shih Shan, near Min Hou, Fukien Province.' *KKHP*, 10, 1955.

HSIA NAI, 'Excavations at Ssŭ Wa Shan, Lin T'ao, Kansu.' *KKHP*, 4, 1949 (Chinese).

HSIA NAI and WU LIANG-TS'AI. 'Prehistoric Remains in the vicinity of Lanchou, Kansu Province.' *KKHP*, 5, 1951 (Chinese).

INSTITUTE OF ARCHAEOLOGY OF THE ACADEMY OF SCIENCES, PEKING, 'Collected Archaeological Papers of Liang Ssŭ-yung.' *Special Archaeological Series*, B, No 5, 1959 (Chinese: Liang-Ssû-yung K'ao Ku Lun Chi).

INSTITUTE OF HISTORY AND PHILOLOGY, ACADEMIA SINICA, 'Ch'eng Tzŭ Yai. The Black Pottery Culture Site at Lung Shan Chen in Li Ch'eng Hsien, Shantung Province.' Peking, 1934 (Chinese, translated by K. Starr as *Yale University Publications in Anthropology*, No 52, 1956).

LIANG SSŬ-YUNG, 'The Lung Shan Culture.' *KKHP*, 7, 1954 (Chinese).

LIU TUNG-YUAN, 'Archaeological Survey of the Neolithic Site of the Lung Shan Culture at Liang Ch'eng Chen, Jih Chao, Shantung Province.' *KKHP*, 1, 1958 (Chinese).

P. TEILHARD DE CHARDIN and C. C. YOUNG, 'On Some Neolithic (and possibly Palaeolithic) finds in Mongolia, Sinkiang and West China.' *Bull. Geol. Soc. China*, Vol. XII, No 1, Peking, 1933.

YIN HUAN-CHANG, *Neolithic Sites in East China*, Shanghai, 1955 (Chinese: Hua Tung Hsein Shih Ch'i Tai I Chih).

POTTERY, TOOLS, etc.

AN CHIH-MIN, 'The Stone Knives of Ancient China.' *KKHP*, 10, 1955 (Chinese).

J. G. ANDERSSON, 'Symbolism in the Prehistoric Painted Ceramics of China.' *BMFEAS*, 1, 1929.

T. J. ARNE, 'Painted Stone Age Pottery from the Province of Honan, China.' *Geological Survey of China*. Peking, 1925.

A. BULLEN, *The Meaning of China's Most Ancient Art*. Leiden, 1952.

B. KARLGREN, 'Some Ritual Objects of Prehistoric China.' *BMFEAS*, 14, 1942.

LIN HUI-HSIANG, 'Stepped Adze, one of the Characteristics of the Neolithic Culture in the South-Eastern Region of China.' *KKHP*, 3, 1958 (Chinese).

N. PALMGREN, 'Kansu Mortuary Urns of the Pan Shan and Ma Chang Groups.' *Geological Survey of China*. Peking, 1934.

G. D. WU, *Prehistoric Pottery in China*. London, 1938.

YIN HUAN-CHANG, 'On the Date of the Pottery with Impressed Geometrical Pattern in the South-East District of China.' *KKHP*, 1, 1958 (Chinese).

Shang

EXCAVATIONS

INSTITUTE OF ARCHAEOLOGY OF ACADEMY OF SCIENCES, PEKING, *Report of Excavations at Hui Hsien*. Peking, 1956 (Chinese: Hui Hsien Fa Chüeh Pao Kao).

CHOU HENG, 'A Preliminary Study of the Material Remains from the Ancient Site of the Yin Period at Cheng Chou.' *KKHP*, 3, 1956 (Chinese).

H. S. HANSFORD, 'A Visit to Anyang.' *Tr OCS*, 1948-9.

HONAN PROVINCE BUREAU OF CULTURE, 'Excavation of Shang Dynasty Sites at Cheng Chou.' *KKHP*, 1, 1957.

HU HOU⁄HSUAN, *Excavations at Yin Hsü*. Shanghai, 1955 (Chinese: Yin Hsü Fa Chueh).

INSTITUTE OF ARCHAEOLOGY OF THE ACADEMY OF SCIENCES, PEKING, *The Erh Li Kang Site at Cheng Chou, Special Archaeological Series*, D, No. 7, 1959 (Chinese: Cheng Chou Erh Li Kang).

INSTITUTE OF HISTORY AND PHILOLOGY, ACADEMIA SINICA, *Excava⁄ tions at Anyang*. Peking, 1929–1933 (Chinese: An Yang Fa Chüeh Pao Kao).

KUO PAO⁄CHÜN, 'Excavations at Yin Hsü in 1950.' *KKHP*, 5, 1951 (Chinese).

SHIH CHANG⁄JU, 'Important Recent Finds at Yin Hsü, and on the Stratigraphy at Hsiao T'un.' *KKHP*, 2, 1947 (Chinese).

MA TE⁄CHIH, COU YUNG⁄CHEN, YÜN⁄P'ENG, 'Excavations in 1953 at Ta Ssǔ K'ung Village near Anyang. *KKHP*, 9, 1955 (Chinese).

NANKING NATIONAL MUSEUM, 'First and Second Excavations at Pai Yin Yang Ying.' Nanking. *KKHP*, 1, 1958 (Chinese).

SUEJI UMEHARA, *Ancient Treasures Found at Anyang Yin Sites*. Kyoto, 1940 (Japanese: Kanan An⁄yō Ihō).

SUEJI UMEHARA, *Studies on Relics from Anyang, Honan*. Kyoto, 1941 (Japanese: Ka⁄nan An⁄yō Imotsu no Kenkyū).

SUEJI UMEHARA, *Catalogue of the Impressions of Wooden Objects Discovered in Yin Tombs*. Kyoto, 1959 (Japanese: Inbo Hakken Mokki In⁄ei Zuroku).

W. C. WHITE, *Bronze Culture of Ancient China*. Toronto, 1956.

STUDIES OF BRONZE VESSELS

P. ACKERMAN, *Ritual Bronzes of Ancient China*. New York, 1945.

L. BACHHOFER, 'The Evolution of Shang and Early Chou Bronzes.' *The Bulletin of Art*, June 1944, 107–16.

CH'EN MENG⁄CHIA, 'Bronzes of the Yin Dynasty.' *KKHP*, 7, 1954 (Chinese) of Hsi Pei Kang.

HAYASHI MINAO, 'On Dragons Appearing on Yin and Chou.' *Tōhō Gakuhō (Kyoto)*, No 23, 1953 (Japanese).

JUNG KENG, 'An Account of the Bronze Vessels of Yin and Chou.' *Institute of Archaeology of the Academy of Sciences, Peking. Special Archaeo⁄*

logical Series, C, No 2, 1958 (Chinese: Yin Chou Ch'ing T'ung Ch'i T'ung Lun).

JUNG KENG, *A Comprehensive Study of the Ritual Vessels of Shang and Chou*. Peking, 1941 (Chinese: Shang Chou Ti Ch'i T'ung K'ao).

B. KARLGREN, 'Yin and Chou in Chinese Bronzes.' *BMFEAS*, 8, 1936.

B. KARLGREN, 'New Studies in Chinese Bronzes.' *BMFEAS*, 9, 1937.

B. KARLGREN, 'Some Early Chinese Bronze Masters.' *BMFEAS*, 16, 1944.

B. KARLGREN, 'Once Again the A and B Styles in Yin Ornamentation.' *BMFEAS*, 18, 1946.

LI CHI, 'Bronze Vessels from Hsiao T'un.' *KKHP*, 3, 4, 1948–9.

B. KARLGREN, 'Notes on the Grammar of Early Chinese Bronze Decor.' *BMFEAS*, 23, 1951.

M. LOEHR, 'The Bronze Styles of the Anyang Period.' *Archives of the Chinese Art Society of America*, VII, 1953, 42–8.

SEIICHI MIZUNO, 'Problems of Dating Shang Bronzes.' *Tōhō Gakuhō (Kyoto)*, No 23, 1953 (Japanese).

H. PLENDERLEITH, 'Technical notes on Chinese bronzes.' *Tr OCS*, 1938–9.

W. P. YETTS, 'Notes on Some Chinese Bronzes.' *Tr OCS*, 1942–3.

YOSHIDA TERUKUNI, 'A Note on Yin Art.' *Tōhō Gakuhō (Kyoto)*, No 23, 1953 (Japanese).

WEAPONS

HAYASHI MINAO, 'Chariots of Ancient China in the pre-Ch'in Period.' *Tōhō Gakuhō*, Vol. 29, 1959, pp. 155–284 (Japanese: Chūgoku Senshin Jidai no Basha).

B. KARLGREN, 'Some Weapons and Tools of the Yin Dynasty.' *BMFEAS*, 17, 1945.

OKAZAKI KEI, 'On the (Shang) Axe and Spear-head'. *Tōhō Gakuhō (Kyoto)*, No 23, 1953 (Japanese).

ARTS AND TECHNOLOGY

AMANO MOTONOSUKE, 'Some Problems of Yin Industry.' *Tōhō Gakuhō (Kyoto)*, No 23, 1953 (Japanese).

CHENG TE⁄K'UN, 'The Carving of Jade in the Shang Period.' *TrOCS*, 1954–5.

L. C. HOPKINS, 'The Caschrom and the Lei⁄ssŭ.' *JRAS*, 1935, 707–16; 1936, 45–54.

O. KARLBECK, 'Anyang Marble Sculptures.' *BMFEAS*, 7, 1935.

O. KARLBECK, 'Anyang Moulds.' *BMFEAS*, 7, 1935.

V. SYLWAN, 'Silk from the Yin Dynasty.' *BMFEAS*, 9, 1937.

SUEJI UMEHARA, 'A Further Account of the White Earthenware Vessels from Anyang, Honan.' *Shinagaku*, Vol. 9, No 4, November 1939, 545–88 (Japanese: Ka⁄nan⁄shō An⁄yō Shutsudo Hakushoku Doki Sairon).

W. C. WHITE, *Bone Culture of Ancient China*. Toronto, 1945.

ORACLE SENTENCES

CH'EN MENG⁄CHIA, *A Comprehensive Account of the Oracle Texts from Yin Hsü*. Peking, 1956 (Chinese: Yin Hsu Pu Ts'un Tsung Shu).

L. C. HOPKINS, 'Archaic Sons and Grandsons.' *JRAS*, 1934, 57–84.

L. C. HOPKINS, 'Where the Rainbow Ends.' *JRAS*, 1931, 603–12.

MISCELLANEOUS

C. BISHOP, 'The Chronology of Ancient China.' *JAOS*, LIII, 1933, 232–47.

K. JETTMAR, 'The Karasuk Culture and Its South⁄Eastern Affinities.' *BMFEAS*, 22, 1950.

Chou

EXCAVATIONS (*a*) Earlier Chou Dynasty

AN CHIH⁄MIN, 'Excavations at Chia Ku Chuang, T'ang Shan, Hopei Province.' *KKHB*, 6, 1953.

AN CHIH⁄MIN, 'Stone Coffin Burials at T'ang Shan.' *KKHP*, 7, 1954 (Chinese).

ANHUI PROVINCE BUREAU OF CULTURE, 'Excavations of Two Western Chou Tombs at T'un Ch'i, Southern Anhui Province.' *KKHP*, 4, 1959 (Chinese).

KAO CHO'Ü-HSÜN, 'The Problem of the Flexed Burials on the Lower Course of the Yellow River.' *KKHP*, 2, 1947 (Chinese).

KUO PAO-CHÜN, 'Excavation of Ancient Tombs at Hsin Ts'un in Chun Hsien, Honan.' *KKHP*, 1, 1946 (Chinese).

KUO PAO-CHÜN et al., 'Report of the Excavations made at the Western Suburb of Lo Yang, Spring 1954.' *KKHP*, 2, 1956 (Chinese).

INSTITUTE OF ARCHAEOLOGY OF THE ACADEMY OF SCIENCES, PEKING, 'A Cemetery of the State of Kuo at Shang Ts'un Ling, Honan Province.' *Special Archaeological Series*, 4, No. 10, 1959.

SHENSI PROVINCE CULTURAL PROPERTIES COMMISSION. 'Excavation of a Western Chou Tomb at P'u Tu Ts'un, near Ch'ang An.' *KKHP*, 1957, 1 (Chinese).

SHIH HSING-PANG, 'Excavation of a Western Chou Tomb at P'u Tu Ts'un, near Ch'ang An.' *KKHP*, 8, 1954 (Chinese).

EXCAVATIONS (*b*) Later Chou Dynasty

EGAMI NAMIO and MIZUNO SEIICHI, 'Inner Mongolia and the Region of the Great Wall.' *Archaeologia Orientalis*, Series B, Vol. I, Kyoto, 1935 (Japanese, with English summary).

FENG HAN-CHI, YANG YU-JEN, WANG CHIA-YU, 'Boat-Shaped coffin graves in Szechwan Province.' *KKHP*, 2, 1958 (Chinese).

HUNAN PROVINCIAL MUSEUM, 'The Ch'u Tombs of Chan'g Sha, Hunan Province.' *KKHP*, 1, 1959 (Chinese).

INSTITUTE OF ARCHAEOLOGY OF THE ACADEMY OF SCIENCES, PEKING, 'Material from the Tomb of the Marquis of Ts'ai at Shou Hsien.' *Special Archaeological Series*, B, No 5, 1956 (Chinese: Shou Hsien Ts'ai Hou Ch'u T'u I Wu).

INSTITUTE OF ARCHAEOLOGY OF THE ACADEMY OF SCIENCES, PEKING, 'Report on Excavations at Ch'ang Sha.' *Special Archaeological Series*, D, No. 2, 1957 (Chinese: Ch'ang Sha Fa Chüeh Pao Kao).

KOMAI KAZUCHIKA, 'The Remains of Chü Fu in Lu State.' *Archaeological Institute of the Department of Literature of Tokyo University*. Tokyo, 1951 (Japanese: Kyokufu Rojo no Iseki).

KUO MO-JO, 'The Dating of a Royal Tomb of the Ts'ai State at Shou Hsien, Anhui Province.' *KKHP*, 1, 1956 (Chinese).

SHANSI PROVINCE CULTURAL PROPERTIES COMMISSION, 'Excavations of Ancient Tombs at Fen Shin Ling, near Ch'ang Chih, Shansi Province.' *KKHP*, 1, 1957 (Chinese).

SUEJI UMEHARA, *Selections from the Ancient Tombs at Chin Ts'un, Loyang.* Kyoto, 1937 (Japanese: Rakuyō Kinson Koba Shūei).

WANG CHUNG-CHU, 'Tombs of the warring States Period in the vicinity of Shao Kou near Loyang.' *KKHP*, 8, 1954 (Chinese).

W. C. WHITE, *Tombs of Old Loyang.* Shanghai, 1934.

HARADA YOSHITO, 'Tan Han. Excavations at the Ruins of the Capital of Chao in the Contending States Period.' *Archaeologia Orientalis*, Series B, Vol. VII, Kyoto, 1954 (Japanese, with English summary).

YUNNAN PROVINCIAL MUSEUM, *The Group of Ancient Tombs at Shih Chai Shan, near Chin Ning, Yunnan Province*, Peking, 1959 (Chinese).

BRONZE INSCRIPTIONS AND CHRONOLOGY

CH'EN MENG-CHIA, *A Study of the Chronology of the Western Cho Period.* Shanghai, 1945, 2nd ed. 1955 (Chinese: Hsi Chou Nien Tai Kao).

CH'EN MENG-CHIA, 'Chronology of Bronze Vessels of Western Chou.' *KKHP*, 9, 1955–6 (Chinese).

H. G. CREEL, 'Bronze inscriptions of the Western Chou Dynasts as Historical Documents'. *JAOS*, LVI, 1936, 335–48.

KUO MO-JO, *Corpus of inscriptions on bronze of both Chou periods, with illustrations and interpretation.* Peking, 2nd ed. 1958 (Chinese: Liang Chou Chin Wen Tz'ŭ Ta Hsi T'un Su K'ao Shih).

TOOLS AND WEAPONS

CHAN-CH'IU HUANG, 'Iron Objects of the Warring States and the Han Period found in Recent Years.' *KKHP*, 3, 1958 (Chinese).

O. JANSE, 'Quelques Antiquités Chinoises d'un Caractère Hallstattien.' *BMFEAS*, 2, 1930.

O. JANSE, 'Notes sur quelques epées anciennes trouvées en Chine.' *BMFEAS*, 2, 1930.

SAN T'ING-LI, 'Metallographical examination of some iron implements from the excavations at Hui Hsien, Honan Province, 1950.' *KKHP*, 2, 1956 (Chinese).

ARTS AND TECHNOLOGY

CHOU CHAO⁄HSIANG, 'Pottery of the Chou Dynasty.' *BMFEAS*, 1, 1929.

O. KARLBECK, 'Selected Objects from Ancient Shou Chou.' *BMFEAS*, 27, 1955.

B. KARLGREN, 'On the Date of the Piao Bells.' *BFMEAS*, 6, 1934.

KOMAI KAZUCHIKA, *A Study of Ancient Chinese Mirrors*. Kyoto, 1953 (Japanese: Chugoku Kokyo no Kenkyu).

O. JANSE, 'Le Style du Houai et ses Affinités.' *Revue des Arts Asiatiques*, No 8, 1934, 159–80.

J. NEEDHAM,'The Development of Iron and Steel Technology in China.' London, 1958. *Publications of the Newcomen Society.*

PEKING HISTORICAL MUSEUM, *Illustrated Catalogue of an Exhibition of the Cultural Material of Ch'u*. Peking, 1954 (Chinese: Ch'u Wen Wu Chan Lan T'u Lu).

G. SALLES, 'Les Bronzes de Li⁄Yü.' *Revue des Arts Asiatiques*, No 8, 1934, 146–58.

TAKESHI SEKINO, *A Study of Semi⁄circular Eaves⁄tiles*. Tokyo, 1952 (Japanese: Hangatō no Kenkyū, with English résumé).

C. G. SELIGMAN and H. C. BECK, 'Far Eastern Glass. Some Western Origins.' *BFMEAS*, 10, 1938.

C. G. SELIGMAN, 'Early Chinese Glass.' *Tr. OCS*, 1940–1.

SHANG CH'ENG⁄TSO, *An Illustrated Catalogue of the Lacquerware of Ch'u excavated at Ch'ang Sha*. Shanghai, 1955 (Chinese: Ch'ang Sha Ch'u T'u Ch'u Ch'i Ch'i T'u Lu).

R. W. SWALLOW, *Ancient Chinese Bronze Mirrors*. Peking, 1937.

SUEJI UMEHARA, *Studies of Mirrors*. Tokyo, 1925 (Japanese: Kankyō no Kenkyū).

SUEJI UMEHARA, *Study of the Bronzes of the Warring States*. Kyoto, 1936 (Japanese: Sengoku Shiki Doki no Kenkyū).

SUEJI UMEHARA, *Ancient Chinese Mirrors in Europe and America*. Kyoto, 1931 (Japanese: O⁄bei ni okeru Shina Kokyō).

SUEJI UMEHARA, *Catalogue Raisonné of Chinese Dated Lacquer Vessels of the Han Dynasty*. Kyoto, 1943 (Japanese: Shina Kandai Kinen Meishikki Zusetsu).

Sources of Illustrations

Since they illustrate material recently excavated the majority of the text figures have been redrawn by the author, M. E. Weaver, P. P. Pratt, and P. R. Ward, from the Chinese and Japanese publications in which they originally appeared. The maps have been drawn by H. A. Shelley. The following are taken from the sources indicated: figs. 2, 3: Fei Wen‑chung et al., *Chung juo jen lei shih hua ti fa hsien yü yen chiu*; fig. 5: *Seikai tōji zenshū*; fig. 8: *Bulletin of the Museum of Far Eastern Antiquities*; figs. 9, 11, 22, 24, 31, 51, 54, 58, 60, 61, 65, 66: *K'ao ku hsüih pao*; figs. 10, 15, 21 b, c: *Tōhō Gakuhō*; figs. 12, 18, 19, 32, 35, 50: *Hui Hsien Excava‑tion Report*; fig. 13: *Bulletin of the Institute of History and Philology, Academia Sinica*; fig. 17: Jung Keng, *Chin wen pien*; fig. 28: after A. Hermann, *Atlas of China*; figs. 33, 59, 62: *Ch'ang Sha Excavation Report*; figs. 36, 38, 39, 56: *Report of Excavations at Loyang Chung Chou Lu*; fig. 53: *China Reconstructs*.

The sources of the plates are acknowledged as follows: 1–5, 9–12, 33, 51, 52, 59: Britain‑China Friendship Association; 7, 19: Hakuzuru Museum; 6, 13, 18, 25, 26, 37, 38, 41–50: The British Museum; 8: Academia Sinica; 15, 40, 58, 68: Musée Guimet, Paris; 16: Mr Ch'en Jen‑t'ao; 17, 22, 29, 30, 31, 63: Freer Gallery of Art, Washington; 20: Institute of Archaeology, Peking; 23: Metropolitan Museum of Art, New York; 27: J. H. Hewitt, Esq.; 53, 61: Art Institute of Chicago; 55: Kunstindustri Museum, Copenhagen; 57: Museum of Far Eastern Antiquities, Stockholm; 72: after Wen Wu; 73: after *Yün nan chin ning shih chai shan ku mu chün fa chüeh pao kao*; 75: after *China Reconstructs*; 76: after *Ch'ang Sha Excavation Report*.

3

4

5

6

9

10

12

13

14

15

16

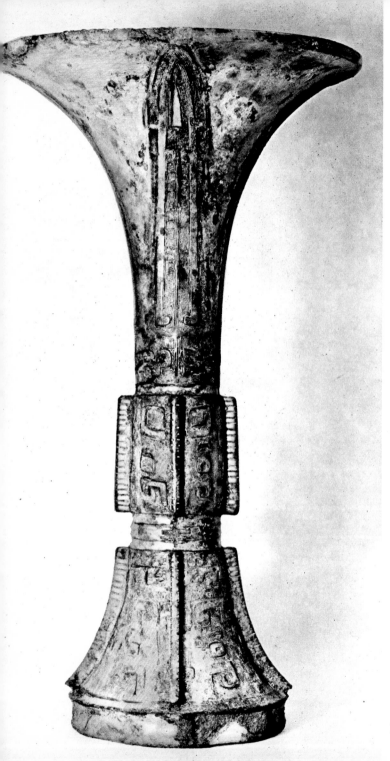

18

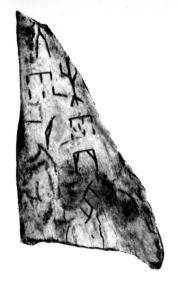

24

25

28

9

32

33

34

35

36

37

38

39

40

41

42

43

44

45

46

4

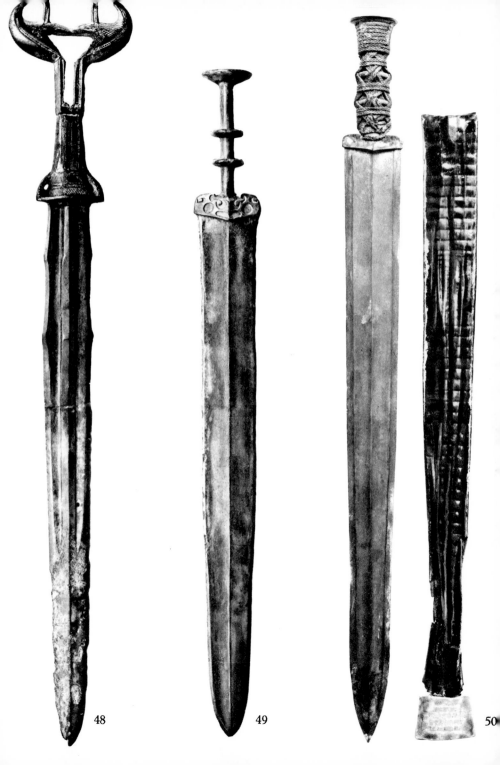

48 49 50

51

52

54

56

57

58

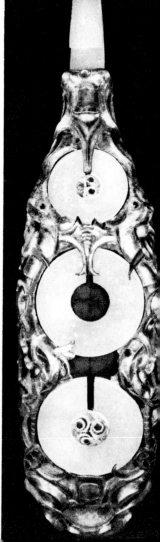

59

64

65

67

66

68

69

70

71

72

73

74

75

76

77

Notes on the Plates

1 Excavations in progress on the neolithic village site at Pan P'o Ts'un, Shensi. The floor was sunk a little below ground level. Ovens and storage spaces are dug in the earth. Yang Shao neolithic culture.

2 Foundations of round huts excavated at Pan P'o Ts'un, Shensi. A central fire-place and post holes of the structure are clearly visible. Clay fallen from the roofing strews the floor. Yang Shao neolithic culture.

3 Grave with flexed burial at Pai Tao P'ing, Kansu. Kansu Yang Shao neolithic culture.

4 Storage pits at the village site of Pan P'o Ts'un, Shensi. The pits were dug among the houses and retain traces of internal wooden structures. Yang Shao neolithic culture.

5 Painted pottery bowl from Pan P'o Ts'un, Shensi. The painted decoration on the out-turned lip is characteristic. The schematized face inside is the only known instance of its kind on the neolithic pottery. Yang Shao neolithic culture. Diameter 15 in.

6 Painted furneral urns of the Yang Shao neolithic culture of Kansu. The shapes and designs are typical of the earliest, the Pan Shan, stage. The 'death pattern' is visible at the neck of the large urn. The painting is in maroon and black, executed directly on the burnished buff clay. The height of the largest urn is 12 in. British Museum.

7 Earth impressions of decayed wooden objects from the royal tombs at Hsi Pei Kang, Anyang, Honan. Above: impressions of carved and painted wooden vessels, right with inlay of shell (height about 5 and 4 in. respectively). Below: impression of a painted wooden panel depicting a dragon, with inlay of shell (length about 30 in.). The paint is red and the impressions reverse the design.

8 Royal Shang tomb at Hsi Pei Kang, near Anyang, Honan (Tomb No 1002). The lateral arms of the cruciform pit are approximately equal in size to those shown in the picture.

O

9 Central pit of the great Shang tomb at Wu Kuan Ts'un, near Anyang. The bodies of human funeral victims were laid on the ledge above the coffin chamber, at the bottom of which is a small grave for an animal sacrifice, usually a dog. Horses were buried in the farther approach ramp. On the left may be seen *in situ* the stone *ch'ing* illustrated in pl. 10.

10 Musical stone (*ch'ing*) from the tomb at Wu Kuan Ts'un (pl. 9). Length 30 in.

11 Burial of a chariot with horses and charioteer at Ta Ssŭ K'ung, near Anyang, Honan. Shang dynasty. 11th century B.C. Recesses were prepared on the pit floor to receive the shaft, axle and lower parts of the wheels. The charioteer is buried prone. For a key to the contents of the grave see fig. 22.

12 Prone burial in a stepped pit, with burial goods of pottery vessels and bronze arrowheads, at Ta Ssŭ K'ung, near Anyang, Honan. Shang dynasty. 12–11th century B.C.

13 Bronze ritual axe, *yüeh*, of the kind used for beheading human funeral victims. Shang dynasty. 12–11th century B.C. The mark left by the wooden haft is still visible on the corroded bronze. Height 9¾ in. British Museum.

14 Bronze ritual vessel, *tsun*, in the shape of addorsed rams. Shang dynasty. 12–11th century B.C. Height 17¾ in. British Museum.

15 Bronze ritual vessel, *tsun*, in the shape of an elephant. Shang dynasty. 12–11th century. Burials of complete elephants were excavated at Anyang. Height 25¼ in. Museé Guimet.

16 Limestone figure of a seated man found at Ssŭ P'an Mo, near Anyang, Honan. Shang dynasty. 12–11th century B.C. This is one of the rare examples of Shang sculpture, and the only piece representing a person. Height 5¾ in. Collection of Mr. Ch'en Jen-t'ao.

17 Bronze ritual vessel, a *ho*, for pouring the sacrificial wine. Shang dynasty. 12–11th century B.C. The lid is shaped in a grotesque human face, with the 'bottle horns' which are usually worn by dragons represented in the ornament of the vessels. Height 7⅛ in. Freer Gallery of Art, Washington.

18 Bronze ritual wine-goblet, *ku*. Shang dynasty. 12–11th century B.C. Height 12¼ in. British Museum.

19 Bronze ritual wine-vessel, *yu*, Shang dynasty. 12–11th century B.C. The *t'ao t'ieh* mask decorating the neck of the vessel is composed of halves which each approximate to the figure of the *k'uei* dragon, as seen for example on the foot of the *yu*. Hakuzuru Museum, Kobe.

20 Bronze ritual wine-vessel, *chia*, excavated at Liu Li Ko, Hui Hsien, Honan. The shape and style of relief ornament are characteristic of the earlier Shang period. Shang dynasty. 14–13th century B.C. Height 9½ in. Institute of Archaeology, Peking.

21 Bronze ritual vessel, *li*. Shang dynasty. 14–13th century B.C. Height 9¾ in. British Museum.

22 Ceremonial halberd, *ko*. The blade is of jade and set in a bronze haft incrusted with turquoise. The turquoise is laid in cloisons of bronze which delineate the dragons and other ornaments. Shang dynasty. 12–11th century B.C. Length 13½ in. Freer Gallery of Art, Washington.

23 Bronze ritual goblet, *chüeh*, for offering the sacrificial wine. This piece was one of twelve vessels found with a bronze altar stand at Pao Chi Hsien, Shensi, in 1901. 11th century B.C. Metropolitan Museum.

24 Oracle bones. Left, from Ta Ssŭ K'ung, near Anyang, Honan, fragment of bone showing cracks from which prognostication was read. Right, bone inscribed with a question concerning rain put to the oracle on the day *ping shen* of the calendar cycle. Shang dynasty *c.* 1500 B.C. British Museum.

25 Bronze harness mounts, ornamental cheek-pieces: centre, and bottom right, head frontals similar to Shang types. Early Chou dynasty. 10–7th century B.C. British Museum.

26 Carved bone handle. Shang dynasty. 12–11th century B.C. Such objects seem to have been employed along with the bronze vessels in religious rites. Length 9½ in. British Museum.

27 Bronze pole-finial in the shape of a horse's head. 11th or 10th century B.C. This piece was paired with another similar, and both probably came from

a chariot burial. The horse represents the small steppe race. Height 6¾ in. Formerly in the possession of J. H. Hewitt, Esq.

28 Bronze ritual vessel, *ting*. Shang dynasty. 12–11th century B.C. Height 7¾ in. British Museum.

29 Bronze ritual wine-vessel, *kuang*. Shang dynasty. 12–11th century B.C. Vessels of this form, which sometimes have the interior partly divided into two, are believed to have been used to mix the sacrificial millet wine. Some surviving examples are furnished with labels. Height 9¼ in. Freer Gallery of Art, Washington.

30 Vase of white clay with carved decoration. Shang dynasty. 12–11th century B.C. The clay is close in composition to the kaolin of later Chinese porcelain. In this instance it is baked to almost a stone-ware hardness. Such clay was used at Anyang only for noble vessels, which were always decorated with carved ornament akin to that used on ritual bronzes. Height 13 1/16 in. Freer Gallery of Art, Washington.

31 Bronze ritual wine-vessel, *yu*. Late 11th or early 10th century B.C. Height 20 in. Freer Gallery of Art, Washington.

32 Bronze ritual vessel, *ting*. 8th century B.C. The figure used in the decoration is derived from a stylized bird motif introduced into the bronze ornament some two centuries earlier. Height 12 in. Formerly in the Palace Museum, Peking.

33 Bronze ritual vessel, *kuei*, excavated at Yen Tun Shan, Kiangsu. Late 11th century B.C. For the import of the inscription cast on this vessel see page 119. Height 6⅛ in. National Museum, Peking.

34 Bronze ritual vessel, *kuei*. Late 11th century B.C. The stylized elephant used in the ornament is a motif rarely seen on the bronzes. For the inscription cast on this vessel see below. Height 7¼ in. British Museum.

35 The inscription cast on the vessel of pl. 34, recording a royal gift to the Marquis of Hsing of 'subjects of three classes, the men of Chou, the men of Chung, the men of Yung'.

36 Above: bronze decorated human head as a pole-finial. 10–9th century B.C. Height 2¾ in. British Museum.

Below: bronze harness mount in the shape of a grotesque human head. 9–8th century B.C. Diameter 2½ in. The Museum of Far Eastern Antiqui⁄ ties, Stockholm.

37 Bronze statuette of a serving⁄man. 8–6th century B.C. He appears to be wearing a court cap. Height 2⅞ in. British Museum.

38 Bronze bridle cheek⁄piece in a bird's⁄head design. 7–6th century B.C. Diameter 3¾ in. British Museum.

39 Bronze axle⁄cap and linch⁄pin of a chariot. The head of the pin is decor⁄ ated with a tiger mask. Similar pieces may be seen *in situ* as excavated in the Shang chariot burial (pl. 11). Length 5⅛ in. British Museum.

40 Bronze ritual vessel, *ting*, excavated at Li Yü, Shansi. 6th century B.C. Height 6 in. Musée Guimet.

41 Bronze openwork plaque of tigers, dragons and bull's head, probably a harness mount. 6–5th century B.C. Height 3⅝ in. British Museum.

42 Bronze axe⁄head. 6–5th century B.C. Length 5¼ in. British Museum.

43 Bronze handle of a vessel in the shape of a winged tiger. 6–5th century B.C. Length 6¾ in. British Museum.

44 Bronze plaque depicting a tiger over a deer. Probably a harness mount. 7–6th century B.C. Height 4½ in. British Museum.

45 Bronze plaque in the shape of a tiger. 7–6th century B.C. This is one of a symmetrical pair which perhaps decorated the sides of a chariot. They lay underground against a woven rush mat, fragments of which have left impressions in the corroded surface of the bronze. Height 12⅜ in. British Museum.

46 Bronze halberd, *ko*, with the hafting finial and ferrule which survived with it. Found near Shou Hsien, Anhui. The hafting of *ko* seems to have been effected as a rule without the help of the bronze mount seen here. This is the only specimen known in which all the bronze parts of a halberd have been preserved together. 4th–3rd century B.C. Length of the *ko*, blade and tang, 9½ in. British Museum.

47 Bronze spearhead inscribed with characters inlaid with gold, inlaid with turquoise at the socket, and decorated with variegated colouring of the

metal surface. The inscription is in the ornamental 'bird script' in vogue in the 5–4th centuries B.C. in the state of Ch'u. It seems to read 'spear of Chou Shao, King of Yüeh, for his personal use', but the obscurities of the script makes the identification of some of the characters uncertain. The variegation of the bronze surface was a technique practised in the Ch'u area, and is known from weapons excavated near Ch'ang Sha. It is not known how the effect was achieved. Length 11½ in. British Museum.

48 Bronze sword with hilt copied from the Scythian type. 5–4th century B.C. Length 20¼ in. British Museum.

49 Bronze sword of the Chinese classical type, with hilt designed to be bound with cord. 5–4th century B.C. Length 18¼ in. British Museum.

50 Bronze sword preserving the original hilt binding of braided silk cord; and its lacquered scabbard with carved jade chape. Found wrapped in silk and fitted in a wooden box in a tomb at Ch'ang Sha, Hunan. 4th–3rd century B.C. Length 21¾ in. British Museum.

51 Iron two-part mould for casting axes. Found at Hsing Lung Hsien, Jehol. 4th–3rd century B.C. Length 11½ in.

52 Earth 'ghosts' of chariots buried at Liu Li Ko, Hui Hsien, Honan. The wooden and leather parts (which comprised the whole chariot except the axle-caps) have rotted away completely and their shapes are replaced by a fine compact soil which could be retained intact in excavation. 4th century B.C.

53 Bronze bell. 5–4th century B.C. Height 24½ in. The Art Institute oɪ Chicago.

54 Bronze mirror. The lozenge pattern derives from textile design. The background, with quatrefoils and the 'hook and volute' motif is characteristic of the mirrors made principally in the Ch'u state. 3rd century B.C. Diameter 8½ in. British Museum.

55 Bronze coffin handle with escutcheon in the shape of a *t'ao t'ieh*. 5–4th century B.C. Height 8½ in. Kunstindusti Museum, Copenhagen.

56 Gilt openwork dagger handle, composed of interlocked dragons. 4th century B.C. Length 4⅜ in. British Museum.

57 Bronze tiger. 5–4th century B.C. Length 5 in. Museum of Far Eastern Antiquities, Stockholm.

58 Bronze table-leg in the shape of a demon, inlaid with gold. The gold is provided from foil, even in the narrow lines of the design, and is fixed by shallow incisions, undercut at the edges where the pattern broadens. 4th century B.C. Musée Guimet.

59 Silver-gilt belt-hook with inlaid jade and glass, excavated at Ku Wei Ts'un, Hui Hsien, Honan. The glass inlay copies the 'eye' beads which were made in China on a western model. 4th century B.C. Length 7½ in.

60 Bronze statuette of a serving-man holding up a vessel, possibly intended as a lamp. 4th–3rd century B.C. Height 9¾ in. British Museum.

61 Bronze flask, *pien hu*, decorated with the 'hook and volute' motif. 4th century B.C. Height 14¼ in. The Art Institute of Chicago.

62 Jade rings enclosing glass ring and boss, on a base of bronze. The glass inlays copy the 'eye' beads of the period. Excavated at Chin Ts'un, Honan. 3rd century B.C. Diameter 4⅞ in. G. L. Winthrop collection.

63 Jade cup from Chin Ts'un, Honan. 4th–3rd century B.C. Height 8 in. Freer Gallery of Art, Washington.

64 Jade dragon pendant. Late Chou. 4th–3rd century B.C. Width 3½ in. British Museum.

65 Jade sword guard. Late Chou. 4th–3rd century B.C. Width 2⅛ in. British Museum.

66 Ritual *pi* of yellowish white jade, covered with the 'grain pattern'. 4th century B.C. Diameter 5½ in. British Museum.

67 Jade slide for sword hanger. Late Chou, 4th–3rd century B.C. Length 3½ in. British Museum.

68 Belt-hook of gilded bronze with inlay of turquoise. 4th century B.C. Length 3½ in. Musée Guimet.

69 Belt-hook of gilded bronze with turquoise and glass inlay. This piece is designed in the 'chip-carved' style, derived from woodcarving, which the Chinese imitated from the steppe nomads. 3rd century B.C. Length 3½ in. British Museum.

70 Bronze belt-hook with turquoise inlay. 3rd century B.C. Length 8¾ in.

71 Grotesque wooden carving of a human head with protruding tongue and wearing antlers. Excavated at Ch'ang Sha, Hunan. 3rd–2nd century B.C. Height 32 in. British Museum.

72 Carved wooden monster excavated at Hsin Yang, Honan. 3rd century B.C. Height 55 in.

73 Bronze spearhead with a frog adapted to the socket. The blade has been cut down. From Shih Chai Shan, Yünnan. 1st century B.C. Length 7 in. British Museum.

74 Bronze openwork ornament, possibly a harness mount, depicting wolves attacking a deer. Excavated at Shih Chai Shan, Yünnan. 1st century B.C. Height 5¼ in.

75 Painting on silk of a woman, enchantress or goddess, with phoenix and dragon. Excavated at Ch'ang Sha, Hunan. This is the earliest surviving Chinese painting on silk. 4th–3rd century B.C.

76 Lacquered shield from a tomb at Ch'ang Sha, Hunan. The lacquer was painted on a base of leather, which was mounted on a wooden frame. The colours, on a black ground, are red and yellow, derived from haematite and Garcinia morella. Late 4th or 3rd century B.C. Height 15 in.

77 The painted decoration of a wooden coffin excavated at Hsin Yang from the tomb which contained the monster of pl. 72. The design is in shades of brownish red, with touches of yellow, on a silvery ground, 3rd century B.C. Length 76 in.

Index

Index

Index